UNIVERSITY OF WESTMINSTER

Failure to return or renew overdue books may result in suspension of borrowing rights at all University libraries

Due for return on :

THE BOYS OWN PAPER

TAKE A COLD TUB, SIR!

TWO NEW STORIES COMMENCE IN THIS PART.

TWO NEW STORIES COMMENCE IN THIS PART.

OFFICE: 56 PATERNOSTER ROW, LONDON, E.C.

Coming of Age of the " B.O.P."—The World's Congratulations.
(*Drawn by* THOMAS DOWNEY.)

THE GOOD OLD " B.O.P."

SONG FOR BOYS.]

[*Words and Music by* REV. W. J. FOXELL, M.A., B.MUS. (Lond.).

TAKE A COLD TUB, SIR!

THE STORY OF THE BOY'S OWN PAPER

JACK COX

LUTTERWORTH PRESS
Guildford Surrey England

First published 1982

The illustration on the first page of this book shows the woodcraft frame designed by Edward Whymper for the cover of the monthly issue of the Boy's Own Paper *and used for the first sixteen years of the paper's life, 1879–95.*

The illustration facing the title page shows the decorative heading of the song written in 1899 by the Rev. W. J. Foxell for B.O.P.'s twenty-first birthday:

> *'As out from Jove's Olympian head,*
> *Minerva nimbly skipped,*
> *No infant but in form and sense*
> *And reason full equipped,*
> *So on the world no puny babe*
> *To East, West, South and North,*
> *A one-and-twenty years ago*
> *The B.O.P. burst forth—'*

ISBN 0-7188-2505-5

Filmset in Bembo 270, 11 on 12½ pt, quotations 10 on 11 pt, captions 10 on 11 pt italics and index 9 on 10 pt
Printed offset litho in Great Britain by
Butler & Tanner Ltd, Frome and London

Contents

Acknowledgments

Above: an illustration from an anonymous poem, The School Band, *published in B.O.P. on March 17, 1883 (Volume V)*

Jack Cox, the author of this book, and last Editor of the *Boy's Own Paper*, died suddenly in the summer of 1981. He had completed his research and written up the major part, but had not finished work on the manuscript. The note on page 124 of this book, written at the publishers' request, describes something of what this labour of love meant to him.

His executors and his publishers express their gratitude to all the friends, colleagues, readers and correspondents with whom he was in touch while compiling this history, and regret that because of the circumstances they are unable to thank by name the many who gave generous and invaluable help.

The illustrations in this book were photographed from original issues of the magazine and are reproduced by courtesy of the United Society for Christian Literature and Lutterworth Press, descendants of the Religious Tract Society. Quotations from R.T.S. minutes and records are used by courtesy of the United Society for Christian Literature.

Jack Cox's family would like to thank Michael Foxell, General Manager of Lutterworth Press; Jenny Overton, the editor who prepared the unfinished manuscript and saw it through to publication; and all whose efforts ensured that this, Jack Cox's last book, should appear in print.

The Editors

JAMES MACAULAY

Supervising Editor, *Boy's Own Paper* and *Boy's Own Annual*, 1879–1897

GEORGE ANDREW HUTCHISON

Sub-Editor and Acting Editor, *Boy's Own Paper* and *Boy's Own Annual*, 1879–1897

Editor, *Boy's Own Paper* and *Boy's Own Annual*, 1897–1912

Consulting Editor, *Boy's Own Paper* and *Boy's Own Annual*, 1912–1913

ARTHUR LINCOLN HAYDON

Editor, *Boy's Own Paper* and *Boy's Own Annual*, 1912–1924

GEOFFREY RICHARD POCKLINGTON

Editor, *Boy's Own Paper* and *Boy's Own Annual*, 1924–1933

GEORGE J. H. NORTHCROFT

Editor, *Boy's Own Paper* and *Boy's Own Annual*, 1933–1935

ROBERT HARDING

Editor, *Boy's Own Paper*, 1935–1942
Editor, *Boy's Own Annual*, 1935–1940

LEONARD HALLS

Editor, *Boy's Own Paper*, 1942–1946

JACK COX

Editor, *Boy's Own Paper*, 1946–1967
Editor, *Boy's Own Annual*, 1964–1979

Above: an illustration by Alfred Pearse from Nearly Garotted, *a story by James Cox, published on December 23, 1882 (Volume V)*

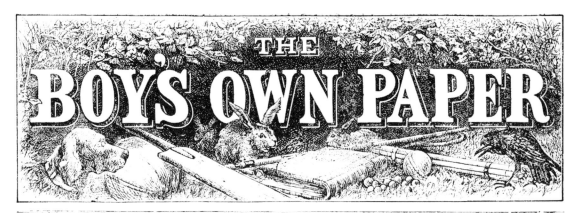

THE BOY'S OWN PAPER

No. 1.—Vol. I. SATURDAY, JANUARY 18, 1879. Price One Penny.

MY FIRST FOOTBALL MATCH.

By An Old Boy.

IT was a proud moment in my existence when Wright, captain of our football club, came up to me in school one Friday and said, "Adams, your name is down to play in the match against Craven to-morrow."

I could have knighted him on the spot. To be one of the picked "fifteen," whose glory it was to fight the battles of their school in the Great Close, had been the leading ambition of my life—I suppose I ought to be ashamed to confess it—ever since, as a little chap of ten, I entered Parkhurst six years ago. Not a winter Saturday but had seen me either looking on at some big match, or oftener still scrimmaging about with a score or so of other juniors in a scratch game. But for a long time, do what I would, I always

seemed as far as ever from the coveted goal, and was half despairing of ever rising to win my "first fifteen cap." Latterly, however, I had noticed Wright and a few others of our best players more than once lounging about in the Little Close where we juniors used to play, evidently taking observations with an eye to business. Under the awful gaze of these heroes, need I say I exerted myself as I had never done before? What cared I for hacks or bruises, so only that I could distinguish myself in their eyes? And never was music sweeter

"Down!"

'To be continued'

Saturday, January 18, 1879, was a memorable day for the youth of Britain. Boys of all ages crowded to the railway bookstalls of W. H. Smith & Son. Village shopkeepers who sold newspapers and such highly respected periodicals as *The Leisure Hour* and *Sunday at Home* found laughing, chattering groups of boys waiting outside their doors, pennies at the ready. This was the boys' own day, when their long-awaited weekly paper became a reality at last, at the bargain price of One Penny. 'Our playground became like a field of daisies, so many papers twinkled amongst the mass of boys,' wrote one reader a quarter of a century later, remembering that happy day.

The cause of all this excitement was a modest, indeed sober, 16-page publication, its format measuring $11\frac{3}{4} \times 8\frac{1}{4}$ inches, from the *Leisure Hour* office at 56 Paternoster Row, London, well printed, and illustrated with engravings and diagrams. *The Boy's Own Paper* was its full title but 'The' was quickly forgotten in conversation, and in no time the magazine came to be known by the homely familiarity of its initial letters, *B.O.P.*

The ingenious masthead on the first page was the work of Edward Whymper, Fellow of the Royal Society of Engravers and a considerable wood-engraver and outdoor artist. As anonymous as the rest of the dedicated team who created those first issues and mapped the road *B.O.P.* would take, Whymper was one of the best-known early Alpine climbers, and the first to reach the summit of the Matterhorn; he was celebrated as the author of *Scrambles among the Alps* (1871). The masthead he had designed showed the range of boys' interests covered in *B.O.P.* Against an outdoor background were displayed a football, a cricket ball and some marbles as well as a fishing-rod, cricket bat and stumps, with several rabbits and a retriever, and a stamp album on the grass. A jackdaw intent on absconding with a marble completed the idyllic scene.

Whymper also designed the cover for the monthly issue, printed on good stiff orange-buff paper which would stand up to wear and tear. His intricate design showed eight insets in a woodcraft frame, with the list of

Above: a tailpiece by P. V. Bradshaw to one of a series of articles on how to make the Boy's Own Gramophone, used in the issue of November 24, 1900 (Volume XXIII)

Far left: the first page of the first issue of the Boy's Own Paper, *published on January 18, 1879, with Edward Whymper's masthead, and the opening of* My First Football Match *by 'An Old Boy'—Talbot Baines Reed*

contents displayed in the centre. Although *B.O.P.* first appeared in mid-January, only two of the insets depicted winter activities! These were snowballing and skating. The remainder showed boating (complete with a lady companion holding a parasol), a cricket match in progress, hurdling, swimming in the river, fishing from the river bank, and climbing the mast of a sailing-craft for the sheer joy of being aloft. Plans for the magazine had been under discussion for a considerable period so perhaps the cover design had been held ready for the great day regardless of the season. It was clearly intended to proclaim that the magazine was lively, progressive, and wide-reaching in appeal. The design remained virtually unchanged until November, 1895, when greater prominence was given to the list of contents, and new sports were brought in—bicycling, lawn tennis, football. With the Edwardian era Whymper's design was at last entirely dropped, and a new cover illustration was commissioned each month from June, 1901, onwards.

The cover of the monthly issue also carried the advertising. On the inside front was a half-page advertisement for boys' books available from the *Leisure Hour* office, the majority being written by the prolific and evangelical George E. Sargent. They included *Rides Out and About; or, The Adventures of an Australian School Inspector: Old Schoolfellows and What Became of Them: The Land of the Mammoth; or, A Boy's Arctic Adventures Three Hundred Years Ago:* and a *Natural History Scrapbook.* The remaining half-page was aimed at parents and originated from neighbours in Paternoster Row. Mothers and older sisters were offered Lyons Silks and Satin de Lyons at wholesale prices. 'No wardrobe can be said to be complete without a GOOD BLACK SILK DRESS, consequently the query so often raised, "Where can I get a good Silk?" is an important one to every lady.' Mothers of *B.O.P.* readers were left in no doubt that if they avoided cut-throat City dealers and expensive West End establishments, and dealt only with Samuel Moore, Wholesale Silk Merchant, in close proximity to the *B.O.P.* office, they would never regret it. Before long, mothers were to be offered carpets at wholesale prices, suites of furniture, curtains, linoleum, travel goods and perambulators. Eighty years later they were invited to buy ladies' models of cycles designed especially for Britain's country roads. At all times *B.O.P.* was something of a family paper.

Mr John Heywood, Manchester manufacturer of school and church furniture, with a London office in Paternoster Square, informed all concerned that he could execute orders with promptitude and on most reasonable terms. 'The care bestowed on the selection of workmen, and on the choice of seasoned timber and other material, the anxious solicitude for customers'—these did more than sell furniture to fathers. They instilled in parents a confident belief that their sons were reading the right kind of leisure material.

B.O.P. readers found their own kind of advertisements on the back cover: Scientific Novelties, such as Bell's Patent Magnetic Telephone (one guinea) and Edison's Patent Speaking Machine (ten guineas); jack-knives and pocket-knives ranging in price from one shilling to four (by post twopence extra); magic lantern slides; model steam engines and model boats, with myriads of fittings; a vast array of foreign stamps from

A deep groan was now audible to our alarmed senses, and we stood still and speechless as statues.

"Let us get out of this," proposed one boy, in a frightened whisper; "there's queer things happen on Hallowe'en."

"Hoot! hoot!" said Jim, but not with his usual assurance. "I wouldn't be skeared at nothing. Ten to one it's a bat among the ivy. Shoo! shoo!"

"Don't go there! For my sake don't go there!" I cried, catching him by the arm; and no great force was needed to hold him back, for now a peal of unearthly laughter rang through the ruins.

"Ha! ha! ha!"

You should have seen our scared faces by the light of the turnip lantern. Before we could move or speak, the sound was repeated in a lower but more appalling tone, which appeared to come from the ground under our feet.

"Ho! ho! ho!"

"Who is it?—what is it?" faltered Jim, the only one of us who could find his

Above: an illustration from the serial story The Bogle *by Ascott R. Hope (pen-name of R. Hope Moncrieff) which began in the first issue of B.O.P.; the episode had a fine cliff-hanger ending—'flying helter-skelter with our eyes shut tight, and a peal of frightful laughter ringing in our ears.'*

Stanley, Gibbons & Co., and a full-page advertisement, clearly aimed at clubs and schools, devoted to equipment for cricket, lawn tennis, archery, croquet and 'every other game known in the kingdom'.

There were no advertisements in the body of the text at all, so the boys who bought that first weekly number got a full 16-pages' worth of entertainment and information for their penny.

What kind of contribution was placed before those bright-eyed eager youngsters crowding round the railway bookstalls and newsagents' shops on January 18, 1879? No editor's name was revealed; no blurb trumpeted the magazine's aims and policies. The fact that the new boys' paper was issued from the *Leisure Hour* office was considered sufficient recommendation for any cautious parent.

Anonymous too was the contributor who had the honour of being the first person published in *B.O.P. My First Football Match* was a stirring and very well-written account of a Rugby football match between the boys of a fictional school, Parkhurst, and their great rivals, Craven, told in the first person by a Parkhurst player making his début, as a late substitute, for the school's 1st XV. Thus *B.O.P.* gave Rugby pride of place in the first issue and at once committed itself to sport and outdoor games, a prime interest of boys in 1879. Illustrated by a Whymper engraving which is a classic portrayal of Rugby's early days, the article was credited to 'An Old Boy'. Who could the talented writer be? He was later to be identified as Talbot Baines Reed, *B.O.P.*'s keen supporter and friend, at twenty-six the proprietors' only concession to youth. The Victorians clearly regarded the wisdom and experience of years as a greater influence for good than the enthusiasm and vigour of young men.

The credit line, 'By An Old Boy', reflected the range of *B.O.P.*'s readership. Many of its enthusiastic readers had left their schooldays behind them, but retained a liking for adventurous reading. The only reference to age-level in the first issue came in the competition on the back page. Readers were invited to write a short essay to accompany an engraving of a lanky youth standing at the front gate of a mysterious house with a 'To Let' sign in the garden. Book prizes were offered for the three best efforts received from boys under the age of sixteen. Entries had to be certified by a teacher, parent, employer or other responsible person as being the unaided work of the competitor. Later, as the response from readers showed how wide was the magazine's appeal, the age-range of competitions rose considerably, with a 'junior' class for readers under sixteen, an 'intermediate' for readers aged between sixteen and nineteen, and a 'senior' class for readers aged nineteen to twenty-three. The senior class disappeared in time, although some older readers always remained among those from overseas.

A first-rate outdoor Nature feature ('*to be continued*', and therefore not to be missed) followed Reed's brilliant contribution. This was by the Rev. J. G. Wood, MA, FLS, a noted naturalist and outdoor writer, who was honoured with a credit line. Many boys already knew his books, especially the *Illustrated Natural History*. The Rev. Wood had been asked to show *B.O.P.* readers what could be done in practical natural-history work with no other apparatus than a common jack-knife. He had a gift for bringing his subject to life, and his own outdoor adventures brightened the printed page. (Some seventy years later, when I myself was Editor of *B.O.P.*, a good friend, the great bird artist Charles Tunnicliffe, RA, told me that from first to last he owed his professional success to the inspiration he had gained as a boy from Wood's work. He used to delve into second-hand bookshops in search of books by Wood and old *Boy's Own Annuals* containing his serials and articles, and could repeat from memory whole paragraphs.)

An anonymous travel adventure about an Afghan brigand converted to Christianity was followed by Captain Webb's first-hand account, *How I Swam the Channel*. Again, this was 'to be continued', and aimed at establishing regular readers. Matthew Webb (1843-83), the first man to swim the English Channel, had performed the feat in 1875, in a time of 21 hours 45 minutes. His achievement was regarded with awe and admiration, and this 'scoop' was the item which won most notice in Press accounts of the new magazine. Webb continued to contribute to the paper, and his notes on swimming in rough seas, published in *B.O.P.* in October 1882, were among his last writings. In July 1883 a desperate attempt to swim the rapids and whirlpool below Niagara Falls cost him his life. Another established writer, Ascott R. Hope (pen name of R. Hope Moncrieff), told a story of bogles and boggarts, the goblins and weirdies of Hallowe'en ('Know ye not whose ghost is doomed to haunt these bloodstained towers?') with a dramatic illustration and cliff-hanger ending—for inevitably this feature was 'to be continued'. The fact that Captain Webb's piece came three years after the event, and that Hallowe'en material was better suited to an autumn launching, apparently troubled no one.

The first long serial followed. Entitled *From Powder Monkey to Admiral; or, The Stirring Days of the British Navy*, it was written by the established author, W. H. G. Kingston, whose work included such well-known books as *Peter the Whaler*, *True Blue*, and *Old Jack*—a book which Matthew Webb had read as a boy and which had inspired him to seek a career at sea. According to W. J. Gordon, chief sub-editor and *B.O.P.* anchorman for over forty years, *From Powder Monkey to Admiral* was suggested and titled by G. A. Hutchison, *B.O.P.*'s acting editor, who had had to revise and rewrite so much of the manuscript that Gordon felt he should have been given a joint credit★. But it was clearly not the policy of the proprietors to credit any member of staff. They wanted to get the new paper known for the quality of its reading matter, and to draw in established authors whose work would impress parents and teachers.

For good measure there was a second long serial, with thumbnail illustrations, from the pen of 'the very popular Mrs Eiloart' (Gordon's description). *Jack and John: Their Friends and Their Fortunes* was largely a study of character, set in 'bonny, beautiful Devon', describing two boys of very different types, yet close friends. This was an item which mothers and sisters must have enjoyed. It was the sixth contribution in the first issue of *B.O.P.* which was 'to be continued' in succeeding parts!

By far the most entertaining feature of that first issue was *My Monkeys and How I Manage Them* by Frank Buckland, MA. All boys either kept pets themselves or longed to do so, and from the beginning *B.O.P.* developed this interest with much advice and information of a practical kind. This account is as fresh and lively today as when it was first written. There followed a second contribution from the Rev. J. G. Wood, this time anonymous, on outdoor sports and pastimes in winter: *Skating and Scuttling*, illustrated with silhouette figures. The secretary of the Royal Humane Society wrote an inspiring piece on, *Youthful Honours Bravely*

Above: the decorative heading of the serial story Jack and John *from the first issue of* B.O.P. *showing cheerful Jack Carstone, aged thirteen, with his 'merry eye and open sunny face'*

★   Gordon, W. J., *The Boy's Own Paper Hutchison Memorial*, 1913.

Won in which he outlined the heroism of three boys who had risked their lives to save others from drowning ('It was an awful moment—a human being left to perish, and numbers in view of the scene'). The final contribution, *Evenings at Home: Pleasant Hours with the Magic Lantern* came as a relief after so much concentrated outdoor endeavour.

Anecdotes, riddles, a puzzle, a poem ('Whatever you are, be brave, boys!') and the picture-essay competition broke up the pages of text. Apart from the tale of the reformed Afghan bandit, the only item of a religious nature was a paragraph on an Old Testament legend.

The new paper intended to live up to its motto, carefully concocted in Latin and placed in an arc of splendour on the cover, *Quicquid agunt pueri nostri farrago libelli*, which the staff translated freely as 'whatever boys do makes up the mixture of our little book'. In my own days as Editor the same words appeared on the perimeter of a handsome gold-and-white enamel buttonhole badge which members of the famous *B.O.P. Club* purchased for a shilling each, from the *B.O.P.* office. The motto was to remain throughout the paper's long history.

Well received though it was, that first issue of *B.O.P.* showed no signs of becoming a British institution. Yet its impact was to be world-wide, its influence to last for virtually a century. Few publications can ever have been as loved.

Right: a line decoration from a characteristic B.O.P. *series of articles entitled* A Life on the Ocean Wave *by 'A Late Naval Officer' which appeared in Volume II, 1879–80*

Chapter One

An Enterprise from which Others Shrank

The Boy's Own Paper was born in response to the demand for 'a good, long read'. Forster's Elementary Education Act of 1870 at last brought basic education within reach of the great majority of children. Elementary schools were to be provided throughout the country. These were either Church schools or schools under the direction of School Boards set up for the purpose. By 1900, shortly before a new Education Act (1902) abolished the Boards, the London School Board alone had opened 481 schools. Although the spread of literacy was gradual, there was a growing demand for reading matter. The expansion of Britain's railway system and the appearance of the station bookstalls of W. H. Smith and Son, over a thousand of which followed in its wake, made newspapers and magazines readily available throughout the kingdom. An alternative to the 'penny dreadfuls' of the day, with their cheap sensational stories and lurid illustrations, was urgently needed. Parents, teachers, clergy and church workers, professional men (doctors of medicine in particular), politicians and philanthropists, all added their weight to the demand.

In addition to the railway bookstalls, there was a further invaluable distribution agency in the Sunday School system. Many children were taught the basic skills of reading and writing by volunteer Sunday School teachers. My own grandfather, born in a Lincolnshire village in 1857, learned to read and write at Sunday School, paying a penny a time for two hours' instruction, the only schooling he had. When *B.O.P.* started in 1879, he was twenty-two, but he bought and read it weekly for some three years. No doubt there were many others like him. Many established Sunday Schools were to place bulk orders for the new *B.O.P.*, giving copies away free to boys as rewards for regular attendance.

A number of those concerned about the need for better reading matter had approached the Religious Tract Society at 56, Paternoster Row, which already had some experience of publishing magazines for young people. Its earliest venture in this field was the monthly *Child's Companion or Sunday Scholar's Reward*, founded in 1824, 'a periodical which has

Above: a line decoration for Straightforward Conjuring Tricks *by Dr Scoffern published on March 19, 1881* (*Volume III*)

THE CHILD'S COMPANION.

Above: the first issue of the monthly magazine The Child's Companion *brought out by the Religious Tract Society in 1824; in its first year 390,000 copies were sold and the profits were devoted to a fund for the distribution of Christian literature among children in India. The Editor, Mr William Freeman Lloyd, an active supporter of the Sunday School cause, was elected to the R.T.S. Committee in 1816, and from 1825 wrote and edited full time for the Society until his retirement in 1846*

conveyed instruction and amusement to many youthful minds'*. It was opposed by many at the time of its first issue, on the grounds that the money could be better used, bookshop trade would suffer, and children would read the magazine instead of sitting down with their Bibles; but it soon achieved respectability. *The Leisure Hour*, a weekly magazine which began publication in 1852, was 'a family journal of instruction, and recreation', 'treating all subjects of human interest in the light of Christian truth'†. *Sunday at Home* followed in 1853 with 'lighter religious literature for the young and uninstructed, and even for the wearied Christian on the hours of the Sabbath not devoted to more serious meditations'†. Both magazines were criticised as being too secular to be proper work for a Religious Tract Society, but the Society defended itself on the grounds that it was endeavouring to drive out the evil of the 'pernicious press' by offering the good.

From time to time the Society was urged to establish some 'suitable and healthy weekday periodical for young people, especially for boys', and its Annual Report for 1868 graphically criticised the cheap sensational magazines being read by young people, and spoke of the Society's wish to see an appropriate penny periodical for 'shop-boys and girls', young people leaving school, and children still at their lessons. It was to be another eleven years, however, before the Society's good intentions bore fruit.

The Religious Tract Society had been formed eighty years earlier by the Rev. George Burder of Coventry, to answer the need for tracts of a 'decidedly religious' character. He and a friend, the Rev. Samuel Greatheed, published half a dozen penny tracts through a London bookseller. Unfortunately the bookseller went bankrupt, which 'led to a considerable loss on the part of the benevolent and disinterested writers'. They therefore decided to form a society which would publish and distribute a wide variety of religious tracts, with a repository 'to which all persons might freely resort, where the opulent man might spend his guinea, and the poor man meet with cheerful civility though his order should not exceed a penny'. On May 8, 1799, Mr Burder put forward his plan at a meeting of the London Missionary Society, and received an encouraging response. A man with a gift for seizing the moment, he promptly invited all the interested parties to a breakfast meeting in St Paul's Coffee House on the following day, Thursday, May 9, at seven o'clock in the morning. Forty ministers came to the breakfast; the Society was established; a sub-committee was chosen to draw up the Rules; and at a second breakfast meeting a day later the Rules were adopted, the subscription fixed, and twelve members (six ministers, four gentlemen, a treasurer and a secretary) appointed to form a General Committee.

For the first seven years, the Society's publishing programme was handled by Mr Thomas Williams of Stationer's Court, acting as publisher, salesman, editor and accountant at a salary of £60 a year. In 1806

---

* This quotation and all others in this chapter for which no other source is given are taken from the *Jubilee Memorial of the Religious Tract Society* by William Jones (R.T.S., 1850), on which this outline of the Society's history is based.

† Green, Samuel G., *Story of the Religious Tract Society*, R.T.S., 1899.

Left: an illustration from The Story of the Religious Tract Society *by the Rev. Samuel G. Green. In 1877, seven years after the introduction of Forster's Elementary Education Act, seventy thousand pupils from London's board schools entered for a 'voluntary examination' designed to test their knowledge of the Scriptures. The Religious Tract Society donated the prizes—four thousand specially-bound Bibles and Testaments, presented at the Crystal Palace by Mr Forster himself. At a given signal, all four thousand prize-winners displayed their open volumes of Scripture, a scene described as unforgettable*

it was taken over by Mr J. Burdett, on whose behalf the Committee rented half a shop (all it could afford) at 60, Paternoster Row, keeping its stock in the cellar. In 1820 the Society took new premises at 14, Newgate Street, hoping for better facilities, but finding its hopes disappointed, returned to Paternoster Row, where it leased Number 56. 'There the Society advanced under the Divine Blessing,' taking on a further three houses in quick succession (Numbers 57, 58 and 59), to which were added Number 65 St Paul's Churchyard and, finally, four houses in Chapter House Court. The buildings were roomy but dilapidated, and in 1843–4 the Society rebuilt the premises. It was by now established on a firm business basis, publishing tracts, sermons, books, commentaries and periodicals. By 1850, there were 4,363 titles in its catalogue. It also opened and supported libraries at home and abroad, and its tracts circulated throughout the world, from Iceland to Polynesia.

By 1878, the General Committee was made up of the Trustees, a Treasurer, two Honorary Secretaries (one of them a bishop, and both of them doctors of divinity), two Secretaries, an Associate Secretary, four

Ministers and eight Gentlemen. The Annual Meeting was held, according to tradition, on the first Thursday in May. At this meeting, on May 3, 1878, Sir Charles Reed presiding, the Sub-Committees were appointed for the following year: a Copyright Sub-Committee (which examined and recommended works for publication) and a Finance Sub-Committee, combining when necessary to form the Joint Sub-Committee. When the General Committee met again, on July 16, 1878, 'a conversation arose on the subject of providing healthy boy literature to counteract the vastly increasing circulation of illustrated and other papers and tales of a bad tendency'*. In the Annual Report of the following year, the Committee recorded the climate of opinion that had influenced its deliberations:

Juvenile crime was being largely stimulated by the pernicious literature circulated among our lads. Judges, magistrates, schoolmasters, prison chaplains, and others were deploring the existence of the evil, and calling loudly for a remedy, but none seemed to be forthcoming. The Committee, fully admitting the terrible necessity of a publication which might to some extent supplant those of a mischievous tendency, yet hesitated to enter upon the task. To have made it obtrusively or largely religious in its teaching would have been to defeat the object in view. Yet it did not seem to come within the scope of the Society's operations if this were not the case. It was therefore hoped that some private publisher would undertake the task of producing a paper which should be sound and healthy in tone, and which the boys would buy and read. But no one would incur the risk of pecuniary loss which such a publication seemed to threaten. A number of gentlemen interested in the welfare of our juvenile population met and formed themselves into a committee to carry on the work—the late Mr John MacGregor ('Rob Roy') being a prominent member—but found it beset by so many difficulties that they abandoned it in despair. It was thus forced upon the Committee to attempt an enterprise from which others shrank.

A week later, after considering the difficulties, the Joint Sub-Committee recommended that the Society should publish 'a magazine for Boys to be issued weekly at a price of 1 penny'†. They added, very sensibly, that in their opinion 'it would be impossible to exclude the notice of athletic sports and games'†. The Society circularised a number of prominent clergymen and laymen, outlining the proposal, and the great majority offered approval and support.

Despite the threat of 'pecuniary loss' so present to the Committee's mind, there were persistent rumours that other publishing houses were working on similar ideas for juvenile magazines to meet the growing demand for good wholesome reading, and a number of periodicals were already in existence. The Society gathered in a score of weekly and monthly magazines of varying quality, including some that had ceased publication within the past decade, and examined them carefully. The three magazines that made the greatest impact on Committee members were the *Boy's Journal* (1863-70), published by Henry Vickers; *Every Boy's Magazine*, published by Edmund Routledge from 1863 onwards‡; and *Boy's Own Magazine*, published by Samuel O. Beeton from 1856 to

---

*   Minutes of the General Committee of the Religious Tract Society, July 16, 1878.
†   Minutes of the Joint Sub-Committee of the Religious Tract Society, July 23, 1878.
‡   The Society eventually bought this magazine and incorporated it into *B.O.P.* in 1888.

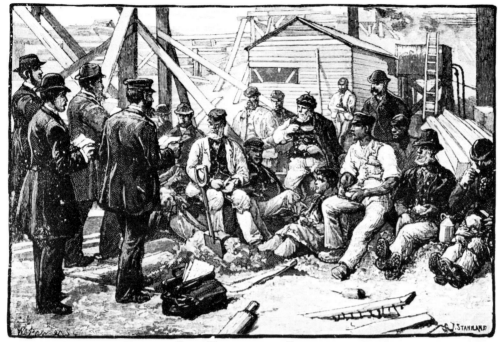

TRACT WORK AMONG THE NAVVIES.

1874. The *B.O.P.* enterprise owed a considerable debt to Beeton's early efforts. He had originally chosen a large folio-size format for his magazine, and wanting to get away from the lurid drawings in the cheap rubbishy 'bloods', at first used no illustrations or advertisements other than a few house-announcements. He later changed to a demy octavo format, by which time he had come to realise that illustrations attracted readers, while quality advertisements kept the costs down. Beeton's assistant and supporter was the Rev. J. G. Wood, the distinguished naturalist whose 'jack-knife' article in the first issue of *B.O.P.*, several years later, has already been described; through the magazine, as through his many other writings, he fostered enthusiastically the practical outdoor hobbies he loved. Wood endeared himself to young admirers by carrying around with him wounded creatures committed to his care by the public: birds with damaged wings, birds rescued from cats, stoats, weasels, fox and badger cubs, a feral cat caught in a gamekeeper's noose, a deserted baby hare—all were gently installed in his safety baskets and cages, given expert nursing, and in due course returned to the wild. Wood's genial personality and gift for lecturing to young people in a friendly, informative manner made him many friends, and Beeton made full use of this in promoting his magazine. It was probably Wood who suggested to the Society that as Beeton's *Boy's Own Magazine* had lapsed five years earlier, its title was available for purchase and its goodwill well worth having. The Society lost no time in securing the title, merely substituting *Paper* for *Magazine*, and no one could have been better pleased than Wood. The title was criticised by one of the Society's advisers, Lord Ebury, on the grounds that it would put boys against the paper, but happily this proved not to be so.

Dr Macaulay, the Society's General Editor, was entrusted with the first

Above: the publishing of tracts was the prime purpose of the Religious Tract Society and by 1874 more than 22,000,000 were circulating in Great Britain alone. This illustration from Green's Story of the Religious Tract Society *shows volunteer workers distributing free tracts to a gang of navvies*

LATE REV. J. G. WOOD, M.A.

Above: the Rev. J. G. Wood, 1827–89, writer, naturalist, and devoted supporter of B.O.P.; an early editor of Gilbert White's Natural History of Selborne, *he was a prolific author on his own account and, in the true B.O.P. mould, a noted athlete—even in his forties he took a regular three-mile run every morning and reckoned to complete it inside twenty-one minutes*

stages of preparing the new journal, but it was clearly going to need a full-time editor, and Dr Manning, Book Editor from 1863 to 1876, and now one of the Secretaries, put forward the name of Mr G. A. Hutchison.

George Andrew Hutchison was thirty-six, a highly experienced printer and production manager, and a practical editor. Born in London in October, 1841, of Scottish parents, he was brought up in the Cockney East End and began his career as a printer's apprentice. At twenty-four he was assistant editor of *The Social Science Review*, and from his work on that periodical emanated his close friendship with doctors and medical workers, which continued throughout his life. A written note found after his death showed that on one occasion he had helped doctors carrying out research into local anaesthesia, and in the course of one experiment had worked continuously without rest or sleep for three full days and two nights. Though never robust (he never managed to pass an insurance company's medical), he had tremendous stamina and a vast capacity for sustained hard work.

By the time *B.O.P.* was under discussion, Hutchison had had twelve years' experience as editor of *Night and Day*, a magazine for the boys of Dr Barnardo's. He did devoted work in Essex Sunday Schools and for the *Sunday School World*; began, and edited until his death, *Toilers of the Deep*, the magazine of the Royal National Mission to Deep Sea Fishermen; and six years before *B.O.P.* was launched, helped to found, and edited for the first fourteen years of its life, *The Baptist*, launched in 1873 as a weekly family newspaper for the Baptist denomination.

Hutchison's splendid wife, née Elizabeth Jane Brown, was to play her own part in *B.O.P.*'s success, for she handled three or four hundred letters a week from readers (Chapter 6). They had two sons (one of whom became a Baptist minister, the other a doctor) and two daughters.

The date on which Hutchison first began work for the Society is not known, but he may well have been involved with its Production Department several years before *B.O.P.* was launched. The simultaneous development of two long series of books aimed at *B.O.P.* readers, *Boy's Own Bookshelf* and *Every Boy's Volumes*, had clearly been planned well in advance. There were over 125 titles in all, covering every possible interest and hobby appropriate to a boy's bookcase, and serious works on natural science and theology 'for older boys'.

Hutchison undertook the enormous task of working out a compromise between the kind of paper boys would read, and buy; the kind of paper parents and teachers would approve; and the kind of paper the Society, as responsible Christian publishers, wanted to produce. There is nothing on record to suggest that boys themselves were in any way consulted about the contents and style of the new magazine, but Hutchison stuck firmly to one guiding principle, telling Dr Manning that it would be a success as long as it 'appealed to boys and not to their grandmothers'. His first specimen number was laid before the General Committee on September 24, 1878. The Committee members, according to the minutes, 'individually expressed their opinions on it'—unfortunately and discreetly omitted from the record. Hutchison was asked to try again.

The eventual compromise was supported by men of the calibre of Dr Manning and Dr Green (Manning's successor as Book Editor and, after

Manning's death in 1881, as Editorial Secretary), two Committee members who had a strong regard for Hutchison and who admired his work; and in particular, Sir Charles Reed, a Committee member of considerable influence, and a key figure in the *B.O.P.* story.

Charles Reed's father, the Rev. Dr Andrew Reed (1787–1862), descendant of a stalwart Civil War colonel who had held Poole for the Commonwealth against the Cavaliers, was ordained an Independent minister in 1811. His service to the Congregational Church was of the most distinguished character. Like his son Charles, he was an outstanding philanthropist. He founded three London orphanages (resigning from the board of one when the governors made the Church of England catechism compulsory, but continuing to support it and provide funds none the less), a home for the insane, and the Royal Hospital for Incurables at Putney. Dr Reed's son Charles (1819–81) was apprenticed at seventeen to a firm of wool manufacturers in Leeds, which had many cordial business dealings with my own great-grandfather, Jonathan Turner Clarkson (1819–88; cloth maker and wool manufacturer of Pudsey). There in 1839 Reed and a friend founded a magazine, *The Leeds Repository*. As secretary of the Sunday School Union, he came into touch with Edward Baines, MP for Leeds and proprietor of the *Leeds Mercury*, forerunner of the *Yorkshire Post*, whose daughter he was later to marry. My Yorkshire grandmother, Elizabeth Ann Cox née Clarkson (1850–1933), introduced me to what she called 'sound reading' from her own bookcase, on many visits in early boyhood. *The Swiss Family Robinson* was a wonderful first choice, a great favourite, but soon we were into the enthralling stories of Sir Charles's famous son, Talbot Baines Reed, one after the other; in this way I came to know about the Reed and Baines families over twenty years before I became *B.O.P.*'s Editor myself.

In 1841 Charles Reed renounced a promising career in the Yorkshire wool trade to return to London, and became a founding partner in the firm of Tyler and Reed, printers, of Bolt Court, off Fleet Street. The success of this venture enabled him to marry Edward Baines's daughter Margaret. The business prospered and expanded and by 1861 he was able to set up his much-respected enterprise, the Fann Street Type Foundry. The father of five sons (page 28), Charles Reed was passionately devoted to education. He was chairman of the London School Board (page 15) for many years; was elected Liberal MP for Hackney from 1868–74, and as such was a prominent supporter of Forster's Education Act; served on the committee of the British and Foreign Bible Society for twenty years; and in 1874 was knighted by Queen Victoria, on Gladstone's recommendation. Like his father, Andrew Reed, he was honoured with a doctorate by Yale University in the United States. Sir Charles believed that all boys should be encouraged to travel, to learn, and to enjoy healthy outdoor sports. He undoubtedly admired Hutchison's considerable practical experience, and was in sympathy with his forthright good sense.

None the less, some members of the Committee seem to have counselled caution. Perhaps, despite Hutchison's wealth of experience, they felt he was too young, at thirty-seven, to be given his head. Perhaps there were reservations about his lack of 'background'—Victorian snobbery affected editors and writers in many fields at that time. Perhaps they felt

Sir Charles Reed.

Above: Sir Charles Reed, 1819–81, a member of the Religious Tract Society from 1864 until his death; Chairman of the London School Board, he was deeply concerned with the importance of providing sound reading for young people, and his son Talbot Baines Reed was to contribute immeasurably to B.O.P.'s success in this field. Sir Charles had the pleasure of writing for B.O.P. himself in its early days. His article Haul up the Rug, *on the popular theme of rescue from shipwreck, appeared in the issue of March 8, 1879 (Volume I)*

his existing commitments were too numerous for him to carry full responsibility. Whatever the reason, by November 26, 1878, the General Committee had asked Dr James Macaulay to 'superintend' the proposed magazine, with Hutchison as sub-editor.

Macaulay was educated at the renowned Edinburgh Academy where his bosom friends included A. C. Tait, who succeeded the famous Dr Arnold at Rugby School, and later became Archbishop of Canterbury. At Edinburgh University, Macaulay took degrees both in Arts and Medicine. In 1858, when he was forty-one, he abandoned his medical career to join the Religious Tract Society as Editor of its flourishing periodicals *Leisure Hour* (founded in 1852) and *Sunday at Home* (1853). He did a thoroughly good job on both magazines, was made General Editor, and served on the Society's committees. It is not surprising that he was asked to take on the additional duty of supervising *B.O.P.* (and, a year later, its sister publication, the *Girl's Own Paper*), but at sixty-two he was obviously not anxious to add to his workload. He was eighty before the Committee decided to retire him; even in retirement, he continued to advise and guide for a further five years, until his death in 1902. Macaulay introduced the work of several medical friends and former colleagues into the pages of *B.O.P.*, with the full approval of Hutchison (perhaps the most famous of all the *B.O.P.* doctors was Arthur Conan Doyle). He and Hutchison worked well together. There was nothing overbearing or pompous about Macaulay, and his tolerance certainly helped Hutchison to develop *B.O.P.* on the lines recommended by his own good sense, experience, and editorial instinct. Macaulay's great contribution was his early zeal and enthusiasm for the new paper and his skill in holding together through the formative years the committees of clergymen and gentlemen whose approval was vital if the necessary finance was to be forthcoming.

At the meeting of November 26 the Committee confirmed Macaulay's appointment and asked that a new specimen issue should be 'laid on the table' as soon as possible. On the last day of the year, December 31, 1878, they agreed that in addition to the weekly issues, price one penny (which they judged would be more popular with boys than monthly periodicals), there should also be a monthly number, in a stiff wrapper with Whymper's full-page design on the front; the inside front and the back of this wrapper would bring in advertising revenue. The monthly repeated the text of the four weeklies; it cost sixpence, but to compensate for the extra twopence the purchaser would, at intervals, receive a handsome presentation plate, worthy of framing.

The Society had its eye on two markets. The weekly issue was eagerly bought by schoolboys, office boys, apprentices and cadets: read and re-read, passed from hand to hand, loaned out and seized back, until it was grubby and falling apart. Family readers subscribed in more dignified style to the monthly; but often they bought both issues—the weekly to read and give away, the monthly to keep for leisurely re-reading and later reference. The monthly was also, naturally enough, favoured by overseas subscribers.

Eighteen days later, within eight weeks of the Committee's requesting the final specimen issue, *B.O.P.* was on the bookstalls.

Chapter Two

Team Work

Hutchison became the ideal managing editor, self-effacing, highly skilled and professional, popular with all who worked with and for him. He was a man of many outside interests: endless work in the Sunday Schools; campaigning for the Royal National Lifeboat Institute and the Royal National Mission to Deep Sea Fishermen; helping to provide foster homes for destitute and abandoned children. In company with many other Religious Tract Society members and colleagues, he was an active Liberal, and became President of the Liberal Association at Leytonstone in Essex.

Hutchison's Leytonstone home, a pleasant, spacious house with fine views over Epping Forest and the surrounding countryside, was named Ivybank. He lived there for the greater part of his life, and it was in his Editor's Sanctum there that he loved to meet his contributors, anyone and everyone who had something of value to offer to *B.O.P.* The walls were lined with bookshelves and adorned with souvenirs and framed photographs. A decorative, coal-burning, central stove made it cosy in winter, while Venetian blinds with dark green slats brought welcome shade in the heat of the summer. The floors were thickly carpeted with rugs and grizzly-bearskins complete with heads. A huge, typical, dustbin-size Fleet Street waste-paper basket stood beside his simple desk; the editorial chair looked as if it would be equally at home in the kitchen. Arthur Lincoln Haydon, Hutchison's successor as Editor from 1912 to 1924, whom I knew well, told me that Hutchison liked to get through his London duties as quickly as possible. Two or three days in the City office and the rest of his time in the sanctum at Ivybank, uninterrupted, was his idea of a working week. W. J. Gordon, his right-hand man for many years, described Ivybank in the *B.O.P. Hutchison Memorial* of 1913. He spoke of it as 'a roomy, old-fashioned house that became a centre of well-doing and happiness, for George Hutchison was a genuine man and not, like some, a saint abroad and a misery-maker at home. In this house, at his invitation, in 1874 took place the first meeting of the congregation of the Fillebrook Baptist Church, Leytonstone, with whose history his

Above: a line decoration from an episode of Our Holiday Tramp, *a serial story by the Rev. T. S. Millington, published on August 7, 1880 (Volume II)*

Above: the incomparable George Andrew Hutchison, 1841–1913, B.O.P.'s guiding genius for its first thirty-four years; this portrait was published in a B.O.P. *feature,* Boy's Own Writers, *on October 2, 1880 (Volume III)*

Far right: an invigorating poem by Robert Richardson, elegantly decorated with line illustrations, which appeared in B.O.P. *on March 27, 1880 (Volume II)*

life-story is inseparably interwoven.' He added that the Sunday School, of which Hutchison was Superintendent, had 'the foremost place in his affections, though nothing of this was ever mentioned in *B.O.P.* So broad and fundamental was the paper's Christianity that there was never a word to indicate the denomination to which its editor belonged.'

This kindly, stocky man, spectacled and bearded, quiet and unassuming, yet a speaker of rare quality vibrating with enthusiasm, was the foundation of *B.O.P.*'s success. He set tremendously high standards for succeeding editors to follow. 'Nothing but the best is good enough for *B.O.P.*' was a favourite saying of his, yet the magazine rarely paid anyone more than a guinea a page for their efforts. There was something of the spirit of C. P. Scott's era at the *Manchester Guardian* about G. A. Hutchison and his beloved *B.O.P.* Professional journalists in Manchester who saw the distinguished Scott cycling along crowded Cross Street to his office said that they felt like enclosing with their copy a cheque made payable to the *Guardian*. Much the same could have been said of Hutchison. 'I cannot write myself, only edit,' said Hutchison, 'in fact I cannot write for toffee!' But he knew how to attract authors. Writers who *could* write did so gladly, however modest the fees, and the magazine flourished.

Dr Macaulay was ever reluctant to give instructions to Hutchison; he had enough on his plate with the *Leisure Hour* and *Sunday at Home*, and when the *B.O.P.*'s sister publication, the *Girl's Own Paper* (*G.O.P.*), was launched on January 3, 1880, he had to supervise that, too. A curious situation arose here. The Society approached Cassell's in their search for a *G.O.P.* editor, and were more than fortunate to obtain the services of a Cassell's man, Charles Peters, then aged twenty-eight. Peters was to make a considerable success of *G.O.P.*, of which he was Editor until his death in 1908. Yet Hutchison, an older and far more experienced man, had to be content with the formal title of Sub-Editor of *B.O.P.* for eighteen years. The two men were always good colleagues and worked well together on many projects of mutual interest. The Committee made no distinction between them when admonishing either man if anything in the magazines fell below the high moral and religious tone expected in its publications; and on occasion Macaulay too was sharply reminded, despite the fact that he was a senior Committee member, that it was his task to supervise and control the magazines more closely.

In 1884 Hutchison was referred to as 'Acting Editor' for some time—it seems that Macaulay was busy introducing a new juvenile section into his periodical *Sunday at Home*; but the situation did not last, and the title was dropped. Patrick Dunae, a Canadian researcher, suggests★ that Hutchison 'was evidently neither known nor trusted enough, to be made editor of *B.O.P.* in 1879.' I find this hard to believe. By 1879 Hutchison already had twelve years' solid experience as a successful editor, in several fields. In my opinion his sheer versatility and capacity for work dazzled people who had no experience of the demands and pressures of Fleet Street, pressures based on the intensity of the competition and the need to make publishing pay.

★ Dunae, Patrick, *Boy's Own Paper: Origins and Editorial Policies*, The Private Library (journal of the Private Libraries Association), Second Series, Vol. 9, No. 4, Winter 1976.

A
Morning Ride.

OH, is there in England this moment a
    steed
That can match with my Bayard for beauty
    and speed?
Could you see him just now, as we fly o'er
    the plain,
Through the breezy March morn with a
    loose flying rein,
With his small head thrown back, and
    his beautiful neck
Like the arch of a bow, and with never a
    speck
From nostril to hoof, save a star white
    as snow
On his face, like a gem on a fair lady's
    brow.

A morning like this for the season is rare:
There's a feeling of Spring in the clear
    sunny air.
Through the pine-tops above me the fresh
    wind is singing,
From the top of a hazel a squirrel is swing-
    ing;
Blackbirds flute in the elm-copse mellow
    and soft,
Rooks caw themselves hoarse from the old
    orchard croft,
The whole world exults in the strengthen-
    ing sun,
And the thought that the Spring has
    already begun.
And Bayard and I at a hand gallop swing
Through the landscape, as light as a bird
    on the wing.

Away o'er the downs, over
    upland and lea,
Rolling wide, mile on mile,
    like the billowy sea;
Now skirting the bay, by the
    cliff's grassy verge,
Where I hear the low rhyth-
    mical beat of the surge,
And I catch far away the red
    gleam of a sail
Of a vessel blown home by
    the fresh morning gale.

MR. W. J. GORDON.

Above: Hutchison's right-hand man, the indefatigable William John Gordon, who worked on B.O.P. for over fifty years

Far right: an affectionate portrait of Gordon's famous brother-in-law, Dr W. G. Grace, published by B.O.P. on September 28, 1895 (Volume XVII) to mark a year of personal triumph. A veteran of thirty years in first-class cricket, Grace had scored his hundredth century that summer, making 288 for Gloucestershire against Somerset, and had opened for Gloucestershire against Kent in a match that saw him play three full days in the field, his wicket being the last to fall

Hutchison's right-hand man throughout his years at *B.O.P.* was William John Gordon, who worked continuously on the paper from January 1879 until late in 1933; even after his retirement, he remained available to advise and support his successors. He was an absolute expert at covering his tracks, and for over fifty years said little or nothing about his own part in the *B.O.P.* story, while extolling the work of others. I have been unable to find his name in the minutes of the Finance Sub-Committee which annually reviewed staff salaries; perhaps like Talbot Baines Reed, he gave his services gratis.

Gordon's main work was rewriting, cutting, subbing, checking, all of which he described as 'my work as revisionist especially in the field of fiction'. The writers he loved were those whose work required no revision at all, such as Talbot Baines Reed, R. M. Ballantyne, G. A. Henty, George Manville Fenn, David Ker, H. de Vere Stacpoole, A. Conan Doyle, Algernon Blackwood and A. M. Malan. But he took in his stride the tremendous amount of revising and rewriting involved in publishing the work of Jules Verne (page 36), and coped admirably with the prolific Dr Stables, an ex-RN doctor (page 61), whose scribbled diary notes and paragraphs of lush descriptive writing he transformed into smooth, well-running stories, with authentic backgrounds to delight *B.O.P.* readers.

In 1913, writing in the *Hutchison Memorial*, Gordon remarked that readers never knew how much rewriting and revision went on before a story could be published; he named Verne and Stables as examples, and when describing the massive amount of work that Hutchison had put into Kingston's *From Powder Monkey to Admiral*, said, pointedly, that such complete revision merited joint credit; yet he never suggested that the same principle should be applied to his own work, restricting himself to the occasional comment that *B.O.P.* authors seemed to write much better for *B.O.P.* than any other publication, and leaving colleagues at the Press Club to draw their own conclusions.

A family connection of inestimable value lay in the fact that Gordon was related by marriage to the world's most renowned cricketer, Dr W. G. Grace, and was his friend, confidant, accountant, and collaborator in all his cricket writings. Gordon's wife, née Marian Grace Day, was the younger sister of Grace's wife Agnes Nicholls Day; and as Agnes and Marian were first cousins of the Grace family, the connection was particularly close. Gordon's first written contribution to *B.O.P.* appeared on July 3, 1880, a date he vividly recalled in later life, and was a biographical sketch of his brother-in-law ('the very leviathan of scoring'), introducing the series of articles, *Cricket and How to Excel in it*, by the unequalled Dr Grace, which were to follow.

Apart from writing for *B.O.P.* and for Macaulay's *Leisure Hour*, Gordon produced an extensive list of books which were published by Frederick Warne and Simpkin Marshall. His remarkable output included biographies; gazetteers; reference books on British wild birds, wild flowers, butterflies, shells, fossils, coins, stamps, medals, aquaria, woodland, etc.; and a stream of children's Christmas annuals; all making him a valuable asset to any publishing house. Among his most successful books were his colourful story *The Captain General*, which described the

No. 872.—Vol. XVII.   SATURDAY, SEPTEMBER 28, 1895.   Price One Penny.
[ALL RIGHTS RESERVED.]

"On the Bat's back I do fly"

(*With the B.O.P.'s heartiest congratulations to* DR. W. G. GRACE.)

attempts by the Dutch to colonise 'New Holland'; *Flags of the World*, published by Warne in 1915, and still going well, revised by later editors, half a century later; and *Birthday Flowers: Their Language and Legends*, published by Chatto and Windus in 1883, and now frequently sought in old bookshops by collectors.

Like the sound and reliable writer he was, Gordon believed in hiding his many lights under bushels. He could not have been more self-effacing. 'Fleet Street's walking encyclopedia' they called him in the Press Club and he would gladly help anyone at any time, digging into the *B.O.P.* files (said to be the best in Fleet Street) or into Hutchison's *magnum opus*, his own manuscript editorial dictionary meticulously compiled over 35 years and containing more than 18,000 entries★. Professionals in Fleet Street often wondered why Gordon did not apply for a post as editor with some other magazine; one day in the Press Club in 1917 he was asked this very question and replied frankly, 'It has never occurred to me.' How characteristically modest an answer. After Hutchison's death in 1913, he went on to serve Arthur Lincoln Haydon, Editor from 1912 to 1924, and Geoffrey Pocklington, Editor from 1924 to 1933, as loyally and selflessly as he had served Hutchison; and died in 1937, in his eighty-ninth year, after close on sixty years of devoted professional work for *B.O.P.* Truly a giant among men.

Alongside Gordon in the early years of *B.O.P.* stood Talbot Baines Reed, third of Sir Charles Reed's five sons, born on April 3, 1852, at Hackney. His eldest brother, Charles (C. E. B. Reed, MA) became a Congregational minister, and Secretary of the British and Foreign Bible Society. Andrew, Talbot and Eliot Reed all joined their father in the Fann Street Type Foundry; the youngest brother, Kenneth, was drowned in a boating accident. Despite the brilliance of his portrayal of boarding-school life for *B.O.P.*, Talbot Baines Reed, like his brothers, went as a day boy to the City of London School, which had a rare standard of success in producing men of letters and language scholars. Young Talbot, known as 'Tibbie' to his friends, was fascinated by sport of all kinds. His skill and prowess in team games were formidable. He also took languages; when he left school to join the family foundry his French, Latin and Greek were excellent, and he soon became fluent in German.

The family home, Earlsmead, was in Upper Homerton, not far from Hackney Marshes. When the Reeds moved a few miles north, to Page Green, Tottenham, they named their new home there after the old. The origins of *B.O.P.* can be seen clearly in the *Earlsmead Chronicle*, a private family magazine started by Sir Charles and his sons. Soon it was circulating among cousins and relatives in Yorkshire, London and Northern Ireland. Surviving issues cover the period May 1877 to Christmas 1879, the birth year of *B.O.P.*; no wonder Sir Charles was keen to establish a national magazine that would reflect much of the fun and 'sound reading' in the *Earlsmead Chronicle*. The *Chronicle* included papers on such subjects as 'Is Total Abstinence a Moral Duty?', 'Dancing *pro* and *con*', 'Verdict on Mrs Grundy' and other topics of the day; poems, riddles, musical

---

★ Two copies of this work were in existence, but unhappily neither can now be traced.

compositions ('Tibbie' is said to have been a very creditable pianist); charcoal sketches, cartoons and drawings in pen and Indian ink; and endless puzzles. Talbot designed the cover, not unlike the early *B.O.P.*'s, though shaped like a Rugby ball! The selling price was One Penny and the outdoor touch was unmistakable.

The young 'Tibbie' Reed was outstanding in an age which had a high regard for sporting achievement. He was remarkably long-sighted, which stood him in good stead in field pursuits, bird-watching, and rifle-shooting. He liked to help his father in political campaigns at election time, proving easily the best chucker-out there was! A powerful swimmer, he was awarded at seventeen the Royal Humane Society medal for gallantry after saving the life of his cousin Talbot Baines when bathing at Castlerock, Londonderry. At all seasons of the year he found time for outdoor sport. In his recollections of Reed, published in *B.O.P.* on February 24, 1894, a school friend described two marathon summer walks from London to Cambridge—53 miles. Reed and he left Page Green, Tottenham, on a Friday afternoon and walked the entire way; punctual to the minute they knocked on a cousin's door at St John's, ready for eight o'clock breakfast on Saturday morning.

In 1876 Reed married Elizabeth Greer, daughter of S. M. Greer (an Irish county court judge and MP for Londonderry). She was a constant source of encouragement throughout his life. His first two novels, never published, were written simply to give her pleasure. Stanley Morison (page 44) described her as 'intelligent and well-read, musical, expert in needlework and gardening, and an ideal wife for a man as active in mind and body as Talbot'.

By the time *B.O.P.* was under discussion, Talbot Baines Reed was, at twenty-seven, well-known and highly respected. He had his family duties at the Fann Street Type Foundry and, as Andrew Reed's grandson, at several of his grandfather's foundations. A member of the Reform and Savile Clubs, he had social obligations in London. He was a deacon in the Congregational Church, and a devoted family man. He and his wife lost their first child, a daughter, in infancy; but Charles (born in 1879), Margaret (1882) and Talbot (1886) completed their very happy family.

Reed's first published article had appeared in 1875 in *Morning of Life*, a magazine for young people published in Edinburgh by Thomas Nelson. It described a summer boating-trip along the Thames. In the autumn of 1878, when Hutchison was considering manuscripts for the projected new magazine for boys, he received from Reed an article of which he thought so highly that he published it on the first page of the first number: *My First Football Match*, by An Old Boy.

Although he had no personal experience of boarding-school, Reed had picked up a lot of information from Cambridge friends who had been at Radley, and he said quite frankly that Parkhurst, the school where that classic football match was played, was based on the Radley he had never seen. The demand for 'more Parkhurst stories, please' surprised everyone. Reed wrote several more in the first twelve months of *B.O.P.*'s life—*The Parkhurst Paper Chase*, *The Parkhurst Boat Race*, and so on—and was much amused when school games captains wrote to *B.O.P.*, in all seriousness, to challenge Parkhurst at football, or boating, or cricket. In

MR. TALBOT BAINES REED.

Above: Talbot Baines Reed, 1852–93, the most famous and best-loved of all B.O.P.'s *school-story writers; this portrait was published in* Boy's Own Writers *on October 2, 1880, at the start of Volume III, which opened his first splendid full-length serial,* The Adventures of a Three-Guinea Watch

THE TROUBLES OF A DAWDLER.

By Talbot Baines Reed.

PART I.

I was born a dawdler. As an infant, if report speak truly, I dawdled over my food, over my toilet, and over my slumbers. Nothing (so I am told) could prevail on me to stick steadily to my bottle till it was done ; but I must needs break off a dozen times in the course of a single meal to stare about me, to play with the strings of my nurse's cap, to speculate on the sunbeams that came in at the window ; and even when I did bring myself to make the effort, I took such an unconscionable time to consume a spoonful that the next meal was well-nigh due before I had made an end of a first.

As to dressing me in the morning, it took a good two hours. Not that I rebelled and went on strike over the business, but it was really too much of an effort to commit first one foot and then the other for the reception of my socks, and when that operation was accomplished a long interval always elapsed before I could devote my energy to the steering of my arms into sleeves, and the disposal of my waist to the adjustment of a sash. Indeed, I believe I am doing myself more than justice when I put forward two hours as the time spent in personal decoration during those tender years.

But of all my infant duties the one I dawdled over most was going to sleep. The act of laying me in my little cot seemed to be the signal for waking me to a most unwonted energy. Instead of burying my nose in the pillows, as most babies do, I must needs struggle into a sitting posture, and make night vocal with crows and calls. I must needs chew the head of my india-rubber doll, or perform a solo on my rattle—anything, in fact, but go to sleep like a respectable well-conducted child.

If my mother came and rocked my cradle I got alarmingly lively and entered into the sport with spirit. If she, with weary eyes and faltering voice, attempted to sing me to sleep, I lent my shrill treble to aid my own lullaby ; or else I lay quiet with my eyes wide open, and defied every effort to coax them into shutting.

Not that I was wilfully perverse or bad—I am proud to say no one can lay that to my charge, but I was a dawdler, one who from my earliest years could not find it in me to settle down promptly to anything—nay, who, knowing a certain thing was to be done, therefore deferred the doing of it as long as possible.

Need I say that as I grew older and bequeathed my long clothes and cot to another baby, I dawdled still ?

My twin brother's brick house was roofed in before my foundations were laid. Not that I could not build as quickly and as well as he, if I chose. I could, but I never chose. While he, with serious face and rapt attention, piled layer upon layer, and pinnacle upon pinnacle, absorbed in his architectural ambition, I sat by watching him, or wondering who drew the beautiful picture on the lid of my box, or speculating on the quantity of bricks I should use in building, but always neglecting to set myself to work till Jim's shout of triumph declared his task accomplished. Then I took a fit of industry till my tower was half built, and by that time the bricks had to be put away.

When we walked abroad with nurse I was sure to lag behind to look at other children, or gaze into shops. Many a time I narrowly escaped being lost as the result. Indeed one of my earliest recollections is of being conducted home in state by a policeman, who had found me strolling aimlessly about a churchyard, round which I had been accompanying the nurse and the perambulator, until I missed them both, a short time before.

My parents, who had hitherto been inclined to regard my besetting sin (for even youngsters of four may have besetting sins) as only a childish peculiarity, at last began to take note of my dawdling propensities, and did their best to cure me of them. My father would watch me at my play, and, when he saw me flagging, encourage me to persevere in whatever I was about, striving to rouse my emulation by pitting me against my playmates. For a time this had a good effect ; but my father had something better to do than always preside at our nursery sports, and I soon relapsed into my old habits.

My mother would talk and tell stories to us ; and always, whenever my attention began to fail, would recall me to order by questions or direct appeals. This, too, as long as it was fresh, acted well ; but I soon got used to it ; and was as bad as ever. Indeed, I was a confirmed dawdler almost before I was able to think or act for myself.

When I was eight, it was decided to send me and Jim to school—a day-school, near home, presided over by a good lady, and attended by some dozen other boys. Well, the novelty of the thing pleased me at first, and I took an interest in my spelling and arithmetic, so that very soon I was at the top of my class. Of course my father and mother were delighted. My father patted me on the head, and said,

" I knew he could be diligent, if he chose."

And my mother kissed me, and called me her brave boy ; so altogether I felt very virtuous and rather pitied Jim, who was six from the top, though he spent longer over his sums than I did.

But, alas ! after the first fortnight, the novelty of Mrs. Sparrow's school wore off. Instead of pegging along briskly to be in time, I pulled up once or twice on the road to investigate the wonders of a confectioner's window, or watch the men harness the horses for the omnibus, till suddenly I would discover I had only five minutes to get to school in time, and so had to run for my life the rest of the way, only overtaking Jim on the very doorstep. Gradually my dawdling became more prolonged, until one day I found myself actually late. Mrs. Sparrow frowned, Jim looked frightened, my own heart beat for terror, and I heard the awful sentence pronounced, " You must go to the bottom of the class."

I made up my mind this should be the last occasion on which such a penalty should be mine. But, alas ! the very next day the confectioner had a wonderful negro figure in his window made all of sweets, his face of liquorice and his shirt of sugar, his lips of candy and his eyes of brandy-balls. I was spellbound, and could not tear myself away. And when I did, to add to my misfortunes, there was a crowd outside the omnibus stables to watch the harnessing of a new and very frisky horse. Of course I had to witness this spectacle, and the consequence was I got to school half an hour late, and was again reprimanded and stood in the corner.

This went on from bad to worse. Not only did I become unpunctual, but I neglected my lessons till the last moment, and then it was too late to get them off, though I could learn as much in a short time as any of the boys. All this grieved poor Mrs. Sparrow, who talked to my parents about it, who talked very seriously to me. My father looked unhappy, my mother cried ; Mrs. Sparrow (who was present at the interview) was silent, and I wept loudly and promised to reform—honestly resolving I would do so.

Well, for a week I was a model of punctuality and industry ; but then the confectioner

changed his sugar negro for an elephant made all of toffee, and I was once more beguiled. Once more from top of my class I sank to the bottom ; and though after that I took fits and starts of regularity and study, I never was able for long together to recover my place, and Mrs. Sparrow fairly gave me up as a bad job.

What was to be done ? I was growing up. In time my twelfth birthday arrived, and it was time I went to boarding school.

I could see with what anxiety my parents looked forward to the time, and I inwardly reproached myself for being the cause of their trouble. " Perhaps," thought I, " I shall get all right at Welford," and having consoled myself with that possibility I thought no more about it. My father talked very earnestly to me before I left home for the first time in my life. He had no fears, he said, for my honesty or my good principles ; but he had fears for my perseverance and diligence. " Either you must conquer your habit of dawdling," he said, " or it will conquer you." I was ready to promise any sacrifice to be cured of this enemy, but he said, " No, lad, don't promise, but remember and do ! " And then he corded up my trunk and carried it downstairs. I cannot to this day recall my farewell with my mother without tears. It is enough to say that I quitted the parental home determined as I never was before to do my duty and fight against my besetting sin, and occupied that doleful day's journey with picturing to my-those early days he also contributed a series of papers, *The Boys of English History*; an article on the annual University Boat Race, Oxford v. Cambridge, which was to become a regular *B.O.P.* feature; and in August, 1879, a short two-part story, *The Troubles of a Dawdler*, which Hutchison praised for its firm grasp of character and its unpretentious appeal.

Reed was also working on his massive *History of the Old English Letter Foundries, with Notes Bibliographical and Historical on the Rise and Progress of English Typography*. This magnificent book, first published in 1887, and reissued in 1952 by Faber & Faber in an edition revised by A. F. Johnson of the British Museum, was the result of almost ten years' meticulous work and research, and became the standard reference work on the history and development of printing-type in England. How did Reed come to undertake it? William Blades, a leading printer of the era, was the moving spirit behind the great Caxton Exhibition at South Kensington in 1877 which celebrated the quatercentenary of the first book printed in England. He knew the Reed family through the type foundry. Impressed by the skills and talents of the young Talbot, Blades had instilled in him his own deep enthusiasm for the printing and typefounding crafts. They became firm friends and in 1878 Reed accepted Blades's suggestion that he should compile a history of type-founding in England. With the versatility which was his hallmark as a writer, and which is still regarded with suspicion by his fellow countrymen, Reed made a truly remarkable success of this great achievement.

Apart from the monumental *History*, and his *B.O.P.* writing, more fully described in Chapter 3, Reed was a regular contributor to the *Leeds Mercury*, which was owned by his cousin Edward Baines. His main weekly article, 2,500 to 4,000 words in length, covered a variety of topics from the University Boat Race to the intricacies of the London GPO, with serious book reviews and a great deal of information about book-collecting, bindings, tooling, and the whole presentation of books. Reed loved books not for their content alone but for their physical excellence and their cherished associations. Like Hutchison, he had very high personal standards of what was good reading.

Writing in the *Leeds Mercury* in 1884, Reed remarked that 'boys who twelve years ago must have revelled in Highwayman Bob or The Skeleton Bride now prefer the more wholesome fiction of the *Boy's Own Paper*'. The penny dreadfuls he criticised still flourished (as did poor imitations of *B.O.P.*) but older boys were turning to better fare, and appreciated the skill and care with which it was presented to *B.O.P.* readers. It may well be that Reed's knowledge and love of good typography influenced *B.O.P.*'s choice of typeface and quality of printing, and that the use of such innovations as thumbnail sketches, silhouettes and decorative capital letters to 'break up' pages of solid type, owed much to his encouragement.

When *B.O.P.* was under discussion in the autumn of 1878, a young artist, Alfred Pearse, submitted a masthead design to Dr Macaulay. Whymper's design was preferred, but soon Hutchison (whom Pearse called 'the Father of my illustrator life') commissioned a story illustration, and after that the scripts came thick and fast. Pearse was to work for *B.O.P.* for fifty years. His drawings, signed simply *A.P.*, illustrated

self the happiness which my altered habits would bring to the dear parents whom I was leaving behind.

I pass over my first week at Welford. It was a new and wonderful world to me; very desolate at first, but by degrees more attractive, till at last I went the way of all schoolboys, and found myself settled down to my new life as if I had never known another.

All this time I had faithfully kept my resolution. I was as punctual as clockwork, and as diligent as an ant. Nothing would tempt me to abate my attention in the preparation of my lessons; no seductions of cricket or fishing would keep me late for "call over." I had already gained the approval of my masters, I had made my mark in my class, and I had written glowing letters home, telling of my kept resolutions, and wondering why they should ever before have seemed difficult to adhere to.

But as I got better acquainted with some of my new schoolfellows, it became less easy to stick steadily to work. I happened to find myself in Hall one evening, where we were preparing our tasks for next day, seated next to a lively young scapegrace, whose tongue rattled incessantly, and who, not content to be idle himself, must needs make everyone idle too.

"What a muff you are, Charlie," he said to me once, as I was poring over my "Cæsar," and struggling desperately to make out the meaning of a phrase—"what a muff you are, to be grinding away like that. Why don't you use a crib?"

"What's a crib?" I inquired.

"What, don't you know what a crib is? It's a translation. I've got one. I'll lend it to you, and you will be able to do your 'Cæsar' with it like winking."

I didn't like the notion at first, and went on hunting up the words in the dictionary till my head ached. But next evening he pulled the "crib" out of his pocket and showed it to me. I could not resist the temptation of looking at it, and no sooner had I done so than I found it gave at a glance the translation it used to take me an hour to get at with the dictionary. So I began to use the "crib" regularly, and thus, getting my lessons quickly done, I gradually began to relapse into my habits of dawdling.

Instead of preparing my lessons steadily, I now began to put off preparation till the last moment, and then galloped them off as best I could. Instead of writing my exercises carefully, I drew skeletons on the blotting-paper; instead of learning off my tenses, I read "Robinson Crusoe" under the desk, and trusted to my next-door neighbour to prompt me when my turn came.

For a time my broken resolutions did not effect any apparent change in my position in the classes or in the eyes of my masters. I was what Evans (the boy who lent me the "crib") called lucky. I was called on to translate just the passages I happened to have got off, or was catechised on the declensions of my pet verb, and so kept up appearances.

But that sort of thing could not go on for ever, and one day my exposure took place.

Far left and above: the opening of Reed's two-part story, The Troubles of a Dawdler, *first published in B.O.P. in August, 1879 (Volume I)*

MR. A. PEARSE.

Above: Alfred Pearse worked for the magazine for half a century and his illustrations formed so integral a part of much-loved serials and features that he became known as 'the B.O.P. *Artist'*

Far right: Thirst in the Bush *by Tom Taylor, published on July 6, 1895 (Volume XVII), one of* B.O.P.'s *celebrated narrative plates, left to speak for themselves*

Reed's school stories, adventures by Gordon Stables, serials by R. M. Ballantyne, David Ker, T. S. Millington, Fairleigh Owen, S. Whitchurch Sadler, Ascott R. Hope, John Lea, Paul Blake, and many, many more. Non-fiction articles, too, of course: in 1880 Hutchison sent the little artist to the Oval with Dr W. G. Grace to draw the technical illustrations for *Cricket and How to Excel in It*; next came a series on lacrosse, and after that Indian club exercises with J. A. Squires (Pearse later spoke feelingly of the difficulties of reproducing swift athletic action by means of woodblock engravings). He did not work exclusively for *B.O.P.*—in 1901, for instance, *The Sphere* sent him as its Special Artist on the Royal Tour of the Dominions made by the Duke and Duchess of York; but even then he was welcomed everywhere as the *B.O.P.* artist, one Australian reader riding thirty miles to meet him, and throughout the tour he kept faith with his *B.O.P.* commitments, regularly posting batches of serial illustrations home to Hutchison. He wrote poems for the paper, and designed *The B.O.P. Model Yacht* (he knew nothing about sailing, so he said, but the design was superb, and readers' models made to his plan won five gold medals) and *The B.O.P. Model Airship*. It would be pleasant to know if he played his part in selecting and reproducing the presentation plates which quickly became an accepted feature of the magazine.

The presentation plates are still remembered with affection by families the world over. They proved so popular that although only two colour plates were given away in the first nine months of the paper's life, by its third year there were no less than thirteen in full colour, plus one in monochrome. Some were straightforward 'information' plates: *Our National Arms, Flags of All Nations, British Volunteer Regiments*. Others were group portraits—*Famous British Cricketers, Our Royal Family*—and others again, natural-history reference plates of *Freshwater Fishes, British Butterflies, Parrots of Australasia*, and so on. But those which made the greatest impact were the bold, scalp-tickling, narrative pictures. One depicted a Canadian Mountie standing defiantly beside his dying horse as a pack of wolves circled the lonely snow-bound scene on the edge of a forest ... The rest was left to the reader's imagination. Like the stories themselves, the plates were chosen to stimulate a sense of adventure and to encourage readers, in the days of Empire, to 'look wide'. Some were drawn on commission for *B.O.P.* Others were reproductions of paintings by established artists. *B.O.P.* was proud of the standard of illustration it achieved. 'Its pictures are not drawn by the customary hacks, but by leading artists of the day,' so it declared on July 31, 1880, pointing out that of the artists whose work had appeared at the Royal Academy Summer Exhibition that year, five had been published in *B.O.P.*: J. R. Wells, W. H. Hennessy, R. Caton Woodville, Davidson Knowles, and W. H. Overend (who was to illustrate many *B.O.P.* serials).

Hutchison to select and commission material, Gordon to trim and if need be rework it, Reed and Pearse to advise on presentation and, with their fellow writers and artists, to give the paper breadth and colour: *B.O.P.* became, above all, a team job.

"Thirst" in the Bush.

(Drawn for the "Boy's Own Paper" by Tom Taylor.*)*

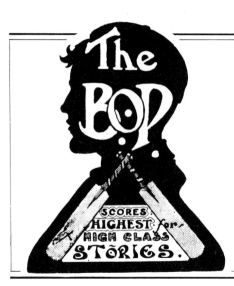

Chapter Three

Tellers of Tales

In the formative years it was perhaps *B.O.P.* fiction that made the greatest impact. Preserved in *The Boy's Own Annuals*, the vigorous and racy tales delighted many generations. In March, 1954, during my own term as Editor, we published a letter from a reader in Glasgow, Michael McDonnell, who wrote:

> While rummaging in our attic recently I came across Volumes X, XI and XII of *B.O.P.* dated 1887, 1888 and 1889, to my delight. Despite their age, nearly 70 years old, the annuals were in excellent condition and quite legible. I have now read and really enjoyed all the articles and stories, most of which appeared to be about the sea. One noticeable difference, though, is the lack of colour compared with *B.O.P.* now. Despite this the stories are so tense and exciting that they surpass anything I have yet read. Could you please bring back some of these wonderful stories? Today's reader would welcome them with open arms

— a marvellous idea, but we simply did not have the space.

The first volume of *The Boy's Own Annual*, containing all the weekly issues from January 18 to September 30, 1879, was published for Christmas that year. Thereafter each annual ran from October to October, and included the presentation colour plates from the monthly issues. Eight shillings, or thereabouts, for some eight hundred pages! When *B.O.P.*'s seventy-fifth birthday arrived in 1954, I compared the contents of several of the annuals published in Hutchison's time with the weekly and monthly issues of the relevant years (at the British Museum), and found that some of the original 'weekly' material was occasionally omitted from the annual, to save space or because new items were written in (November was particularly at risk), although all serial instalments were, of course, included. Readers who had saved their copies throughout the year could buy from the *B.O.P.* office the Annual's title page and index (price one penny in 1881), plus, if they wished, the year's presentation plates (one shilling and eight pence, inclusive), and a handsome printed binding-case (two shillings), and get the whole thing bound up by their local bookbinder. Where such copies have survived, they often include

Above: a line decoration from the issue of April 15, 1905 (Volume XXVII)

In the Nick of Time.

the supplementary numbers which were issued twice a year, for the Summer and Christmas holidays.

The contents of the early volumes, with their strong fiction emphasis, fulfilled Hutchison's and Reed's joint conviction that 'sound reading' must be the backbone of the paper. Kingston's *From Powder Monkey to Admiral*, already mentioned on page 13, was the lead serial in Volume I (1879). In Volume II, 1879–80, pride of place went to *The Red Man's Revenge*, a lively tale of the Canadian frontier by R. M. Ballantyne, who ran Kingston very close in the mid-seventies popularity stakes. The first chapter of *Peter Trawl*—Kingston writing in his best vein—appeared in the same issue (October 4, 1879), and on Kingston's recommendation, so did the opening episode of a new serial by the celebrated French writer, Jules Verne. A short school story by Ascott R. Hope, *The Amateur*

Above: an illustration by J. F. Weedon for the two-part story Jam Roley-Poleys, *by an unnamed author, August, 1880 (Volume II). The Squire's son, a well-built seventeen-year-old, and a fellow Etonian are drifting to their death under the mill-wheel when young Teddy Ashton, an out-of-work village lad, comes to the rescue. An agreeable twist is supplied by the fact that the Squire has turned down Teddy as gardener's boy, saying jovially that he must eat plenty of pudding (bitter words to a hungry lad who dreams of roley-poley) and come back in two or three years: 'I want a stout pair of arms and a good head-piece'*

Dominie, in five episodes, made up the tally; it was succeeded a month later by the Rev. T. S. Millington's long-running school story, *Some of Our Fellows*.

Jules Verne's name was already well-known in England. His first novel, *Five Weeks in a Balloon*, had been published in France in 1863, and in England seven years later. It was followed by a string of bold scientific adventures, including *Journey to the Centre of the Earth* (British publication 1872), *Twenty Thousand Leagues under the Sea* (1873) and *Around the World in Eighty Days* (1874). The new novel, *Un Capitaine de Quinze Ans*, was serialised, like so much of Verne's work, in the *Journal des Débats*, in 1878. As soon as the French galley proofs arrived in London they were rushed to Willesden, where Kingston's daughter translated them into English; her father then revised the story. The original English title, *Dick Sands the Boy Captain*, was crisply abbreviated by Hutchison, who dropped the hero's name. *The Boy Captain* was an entertaining story featuring a mongrel dog, Dingo, whose remarkable talents included the ability to recognise its former master's initials! No boy could resist such a dog. The story ran in *B.O.P.* from October 4, 1879, to July 24, 1880, and was a great success. *B.O.P.* bought the British serial rights in Verne's next story, *The Giant Raft*, and the French proofs were delivered to Miss Kingston that summer. Unhappily her father's illness and death delayed her starting work on them and it was the indefatigable Gordon who dashed out to Willesden and took them over. The first episode of *The Giant Raft* appeared on April 16, 1881, and from then onwards *B.O.P.* published Verne's imaginative and entertaining stories steadily for another twenty years. After Kingston's death, the English versions were edited by Gordon, who had to apply all his considerable gifts as 'revisionist' or rewrite man to the task, for Verne always over-wrote. On his own admission, Gordon preferred the work of another French writer, Louis Rousselet, whose story *The Two Cabin Boys* was published in Volume IV, 1881–2, with Verne's *The Cryptogram*, and whose *Drummer Boy* appeared in Volume V, 1882–3, with Verne's *Godfrey Morgan*; but popular as Rousselet was with *B.O.P.* readers, Verne's reputation stood higher.

Verne wrote for an all-embracing market, but because so much of his considerable output first appeared in Britain in *B.O.P.*, most British public libraries still place his work either in the juvenile section or among the science fiction titles. Born at Nantes in 1828, he had a happy childhood on the Ile Feydeau. Long since merged with Nantes proper, in those days the Ile was still separated from the city by the channels of the majestic Loire, swollen every spring by racing dark flood waters. As a boy Jules loved adventure stories—Fenimore Cooper, Sir Walter Scott, and 'the Robinsons'; he much preferred *The Swiss Family Robinson* to *Crusoe*. He once took the place of a reluctant cabin boy and sailed away down the Loire, but unfortunately Père Verne waited for the ship down-river and dealt summarily with his impulsive son. At length Jules was sent to Paris, ostensibly to study law but with ambitions to be a playwright. There he met Victor Hugo and Alexandre Dumas the younger, both of whom gave him considerable encouragement. He was fascinated by Edgar Allan Poe (1809–49), the American poet and author of *Tales of Mystery*. Some saw in Poe's work the origins of the very horror comics and penny dreadfuls that *B.O.P.* was founded to supplant, but others saw the seeds of adventure writing—detective stories, endless tales of pirates and buried treasure, and in modern times, science fiction.

Hutchison was fascinated by Verne's sheer creative talent and his stories went down well with successive generations of *B.O.P.* readers. The most significant of all the Verne stories, seen from the viewpoint of the nineteen-eighties, was *The Clipper of the Clouds* (published in France as *Robur le Conquérant*) which appeared in *B.O.P.* in 1886-7. The English title, shifting the emphasis from the human hero, Robur, to his invention, the clipper ship, unerringly stressed the true focus of the story and was a brilliant choice. Moreover, until then the contents of *B.O.P.* had been decidedly maritime. Boats and boating, canoeing, swimming, diving, endless serials at sea with heroes in the Royal Navy. The readers never tired of it (time and again they wrote in asking for information about careers at sea, until the Editor's replies became extremely tetchy), but adventure and excitement in the skies must have been a welcome change. Verne's invention was described in detail: the *Albatross*, a helicopter of impressive design, with a flat deck, three deckhouses, and 74 lifting screws built of compressed paper, and driven by electric batteries! (There is a model in the Jules Verne Museum in the Palais de Paris.) Verne's early faith in balloons had evaporated with the failure of Nadar's *Géant*, and he had come to believe that the helicopter was the aircraft of the future. He studied Leonardo da Vinci's notes foreshadowing such a development, and regarded as a significant breakthrough the building of a steam-driven helicopter in 1875 (the latter made a 20-second flight at a height of some 15 metres). *The Clipper of the Clouds* is a dramatic tale with two spectacular rescues, a hazardous crossing of Antarctica, and a splendid climax. But it is poorly told. I. O. Evans described it as 'a brilliant idea badly worked out; my impression is that it was written against time, as though Verne were meeting his editors' demand for copy'. For all its shortcomings, it added greatly to Verne's world-wide reputation.

Did Hutchison and Gordon ever meet Verne? After his marriage to Honorine Morel, a young widow, Verne settled in Amiens. As a young man he sailed the Channel in his own yacht, visiting Southampton, London and Brighton, but the town he knew best was Liverpool. He greatly enjoyed visiting the West of Scotland and the Hebrides. Hutchison took much the same kind of holiday each summer, delivering lectures en route about his beloved Mission to Deep Sea Fishermen and the Royal National Lifeboat Institute. Some writers have suggested that the two men may have met in Antwerp and taken a summer sea trip to Leith. It is pleasant to think of such a meeting, but if it took place, it must surely have occurred before March, 1886, when Verne was shot and injured by his own nephew, Gaston, who was undergoing medical treatment for a severe breakdown. This sad affair left Jules a cripple. For the last nineteen years of his life he could only move about slowly with the aid of a stick. His young British readers, many of whom had no more than a penny a week to spare, clubbed together to buy him a handsome, gold-mounted walking-stick which he treasured. It never ceased to remind him of the hours of happiness his stories had given to thousands.

★   ★   ★

NEARLY EATEN
OR THE PROFESSOR'S
ADVENTURE IN HAITI
A TRUE STORY OF A NARROW ESCAPE.

By JAMES COX, R.N.,
Author of "Nearly Garotted," "How I Saved my Aunt's Diamonds," etc.

CHAPTER I.

ONE sweltering afternoon in the month of June the Iris was swinging at No. 3 buoy in the harbour of Port Royal, Jamaica. We were in daily expectation of orders from the admiral to proceed to Halifax, and looking forward with pleasure to the prospect of exchanging the heat of the West Indies for the cooler climate of the north, when suddenly the officer of the watch, Lieutenant Oakhead, looked down the skylight

Above: a vignette by G. H. Edwards, opening James Cox's two-part adventure in which a genial little professor, armed only with a butterfly net, escapes from a horde of cannibalistic Voodoo worshippers; this appeared in B.O.P. on March 22-29, 1884 (Volume VI)

Good-bye!

A NARROW ESCAPE.

By an Old Soldier.

CHAPTER II.

"Parsons," said I, in an undertone, "there's just a ghost of a chance for you yet. You may manage to get on your horse's back and bolt. It's impossible for me to do the same, so be off at once, if you can."

I think I have already explained that we were in a narrow sort of gorge, thickly flanked on each side by a hedge of prickly pear, through which neither man nor beast, or even bird, could have penetrated, and my being in front afforded cover to any retrograde movement which Parsons might think proper to execute. But how is this? he's very slow in beginning his retreat! Is he deaf? He doesn't even answer. Yes he does, though, and this is what he says:

"Take off your stirrup, sir, and let's give 'em something. If you be killed I'm killed too, but I bain't agoing to leave you to be killed alone."

Riding for Life.

Sea stories, jungle adventures, dangerous enterprises, pioneering in Indian country, tales of gallant soldiers facing fearful odds, all went down splendidly with *B.O.P.* readers and their fathers, although they did not necessarily please the vigilant Committee, whose attitude towards fiction was never more than lukewarm. Macaulay, Hutchison, Reed and Gordon, accepted as their guiding principle the fact that the magazine must

Above: a stirring account, illustrated by J. F. Weedon, of British soldiers flying for their lives in the Indian Mutiny (April 24, 1880; Volume II)
Far left: one of the dramatic narrative plates which encouraged readers to 'look wide' (June 4, 1887; Volume IX)

always reflect the Christian way of life, and the first two Volumes (1879, and 1879–80) kept the standard of storytelling very high. No one seemed critical except the Committee—and by no means all the Committee members were opposed.

Considering the prospects for Volume III, 1880–81, Hutchison turned, in the summer of 1880, to the doyen, Kingston, and suggested that he might write a new serial with an Arctic setting. Kingston was sixty-six (described by Gordon as 'a very old man for his age') and within a fortnight of accepting the commission, in mid-June, wrote saying that he had been seized by what promised to be a fatal illness and feared his work was done. A week later, on July 8, he wrote again, saying 'My strength varies so much that I am very sure it would not do for you to depend on a tale from me to appear as early as the 1st of September'—a remark which indicates the speed at which B.O.P. contributors expected to work. On August 2, he composed a letter to his B.O.P. readers, calling them 'My dear Boys':

I have been engaged, as you know, for a very large portion of my life in writing books for you. This occupation has been a source of the greatest pleasure and satisfaction to me, and, I am willing to believe, to you also. Our connection with each other in this world, however, must shortly cease . . .

I want you to know that I am leaving this life in unspeakable happiness, because I rest my soul on my Saviour, trusting only and entirely to the merits of the Great Atonement by which my sins (and yours) have been put away for ever. Dear Boys, I ask you to give your hearts to Christ, and earnestly pray that all of you may meet me in Heaven.

Kingston died three days later. His letter, with a B.O.P. presentation portrait, appeared in the issue of September 11, 1880.

Three weeks later, on October 2, 1880, the issue which opened Volume III, B.O.P. published portraits of five favourite Boy's Own Writers, 'at the very earnest solicitation of very many young readers'. The celebrities were R. M. Ballantyne and the Rev. J. G. Wood (both of whom had made their marks before B.O.P. was founded): the Rev. T. S. Millington; the 'Acting Editor', unnamed, but with his signature, G. A. Hutchison, among the facsimile autographs published alongside (was this a graceful attempt by the staff to give Hutchison his editorial due?); and Talbot Baines Reed, described in the caption as 'the redoubtable and well-nigh invincible Adams of Parkhurst'—the very first occasion on which he had been credited by name. Reed had made a great success of his short stories and cameos of school life in the first two volumes. 'Parkhurst' School lived, and Adams was a very real character—clearly based on himself. Hutchison was determined that this success should be taken further.

Earlier that year Hutchison had turned to Reed in search of something new. He felt that B.O.P. needed a long school-story serial. Did Reed, despite the fact that he had no first-hand experience of boarding-school, think he could make a go of it? Such a story would need as hero a boy with strength of character, able to stand up well to risks and temptations; strong and courageous in his actions, a Christian in his daily life, considerate towards friends and fellows, courteous to girls and elders—but neither smug nor pious. A modern boarding-school seemed an ideal setting. Many well-to-do middle-class businessmen were sending their sons to such schools in the boom years of the mid-Victorian era. Hutchison himself said (March 3, 1894), after Reed's death, that it was the skill shown in the short school-story, *Troubles of a Dawdler* (August, 1879) that induced him to suggest Reed might try something more ambitious.

Reed accepted the challenge. Although he set aside his mammoth work on the Old English Letter Foundries to write his first full-length B.O.P. serial, he carried on with his duties at the Fann Street Foundry

Below: on the second day of Ralph's voyage up-river from Calcutta, a man-eating tiger rips open his cabin door, and only presence of mind and a handy rifle enable him to survive; hardly has he got ashore than he must charge at full gallop past a trumpeting elephant which luckily turns tail. The artist was Alfred Pearse (July 26, 1884; Volume VI)

RALPH'S ADVENTURES EN ROUTE TO AN INDIAN TEA ESTATE.

BY CHARLES H. LEPPER, F.R.G.S., M.R.A.S., ETC.

CHAPTER III.

WE had only got about three-quarters of the way up the River Bramaputra in my last chapter.

I have not told you what the river is like after getting clear of the Sunderbunds, but it is not difficult to describe, as there is a great sameness about it. A broad, muddy, swift-flowing stream, varying from four miles to a mile in width, or even less in parts. The shores either wooded to the water's edge with apparently impenetrable forests, or else showing a selvage of sloping sandbank from the jungle to the water. Islands of sand, sometimes covered with high grass, sometimes bare sand, breaking up the full expanse of water and adding to the swiftness of the current by diminishing the width of the river. In the extreme distance to the left, going up stream, on the right bank of the river, correctly speaking, one has the Himalayas always in sight on clear days, and now and then a glimpse of the perpetual snows on the farther ranges. But the impression created is altogether that of intense and dreary monotony.

Now or never!

MR. GORDON BROWNE.

Above and below: two favourite B.O.P. *artists, Gordon Browne and W. H. Overend, both of whom worked for the paper for many years*

MR. W. H. OVEREND.

and his weekly contributions to the *Leeds Mercury*. His tremendous appetite for sheer, hard work was a wonderful asset.

The full-length serial Hutchison had asked for began in Volume III, on October 2, 1880. It was *The Adventures of a Three-Guinea Watch*—one of the most famous boys' stories of all time. The finely engraved title, with pictorial illustrations, looked too dignified for a boys' paper, but was just the thing to appeal to parents and elders casting a judicial eye over the kind of reading matter their boys brought into the house. The by-line said simply 'By the Author of "My First Football Match", "A Boating Adventure at Parkhurst", etc.' The school depicted, Randlebury, may, like Parkhurst, be based on Radley but this we do not really know. The artwork, though not credited in the magazine, was by Gordon Browne. His brother was originally commissioned to do the illustrations but had to give up the work, whereupon Gordon Browne completed it. After that he was kept busy drawing for *B.O.P.* year after year, illustrating among others the work of G. A. Henty, G. Manville Fenn, J. F. Hodgetts and Gordon Stables. His father H. K. Browne, was the famous 'Phiz', illustrator of Dickens. The lead story running with Reed's was *Adventures of a Boston Boy amongst Savages* by the industrious Ascott R. Hope, a stirring true-life adventure which made an excellent contrast. Here another favourite, W. H. Overend, was the illustrator.

Reed's story is told in the first person by the watch itself, an original touch. It is a handsome silver timepiece which travels widely, from school to college, and then on to India, stolen from its true owner, a captain in Her Majesty's Army; eventually, however, he recovers his beloved old timekeeper and is able to tell its story to his children, thus giving him every opportunity of bringing in the drama of the Indian Mutiny and other notable events of military history. The serial ran for nineteen weekly instalments, ending in April 1881. It had an astonishing success. Clearly Reed was the writer the boys wanted—and many of their sisters too.

When this first effort of Reed's was published in book form, in 1883, Hutchison, who claimed he could not write a line, so far forgot himself as to supply an Introduction. He wrote enthusiastically about 'the lifelike fidelity with which its various characters, their temptations, failures and triumphs, are portrayed. Every reader must feel that these boys, at least, are no pasteboard figures manipulated by the writer for a given purpose, but healthy, flesh and blood lads of precisely the kind, for good or evil, one meets all around, and rubs shoulders with day by day in school and college, as well as in the great hurly-burly of our present-day cities.'

Even better was *The Fifth Form at St Dominic's* which followed in Volume IV, a story that gained a world reputation for Talbot Baines Reed and is probably his most famous and best-known book. Hutchison made the excellent script as attractive as possible, with artwork by Gordon Browne and H. M. Paget, elder brother of the artist who depicted Sherlock Holmes and Dr Watson. Reed now set to work, and in fourteen years published a dozen long *B.O.P.* serials, in addition to three juvenile novels: *Follow My Leader* (1885), *Roger Ingleton Minor* (1889) and *Kilgorman* (1894). The order of publication in *B.O.P.* was as follows: *The Adventures of a Three-Guinea Watch* (serialised 1880–81), *The*

WHEN I awoke next morning Johnny told me that the bullocks had again rambled off during the night, and that Ned and Dilly had gone to bring them back; so I had plenty of time to run down to the lake and have

"It was too much like hitting a man when he is down."

Fifth Form at St Dominic's (serialised 1881–2), *My Friend Smith* (serialised 1882–3), *Willoughby Captains* (serialised 1883–4), *Reginald Cruden* (serialised 1885), *A Dog with a Bad Name* (serialised 1886–7), *The Master of the Shell* (serialised 1887–8), *Sir Ludar* (serialised 1889), *The Cock House at Fellsgarth* (serialised 1891) and *Tom, Dick and Harry* (serialised 1892–3).

Above: an episode of Harry Treverton, *published on December 10, 1887 (Volume X) and illustrated by Alfred Pearse; man-eaters apart, B.O.P. set its face against indiscriminate killing 'for sport'*

My Friend Smith was set, at Hutchison's suggestion, in a 'lower middle-class school' instead of a public school, and followed its hero to London, 'to deal with the trials and temptations incident to bread-winning'. *Reginald Cruden* was sub-titled *A Tale of City Life*, and was a break from school settings; its young hero, taken away from school when his father died leaving next to nothing for wife and sons, struggled to earn a living as a printer's devil. The background came easily to Reed because he was so familiar with the printing craft and trade. *Sir Ludar* was another departure, an Elizabethan adventure full of Tudor glory. The last serial story was originally called *Dick, Tom and Harry*, but Hutchison felt the names did not run smoothly off the tongue, and he persuaded Reed to alter it to *Tom, Dick and Harry*, thus adding a new expression to the English language.

Gordon's 1913 assessment of Reed's stories was simple and laconic: 'All were good, but the school stories were the best.' The records were lost in the 1941 incendiary air raids, but it seems clear that Reed actually wrote his novels and serial stories in a different order and may well have speeded up the work to win a breathing space for his *History of the Old English Letter Foundries*. In the late nineteen-fifties Stanley Morison, who had access to private papers of the Reed family, and whom I had the pleasure of meeting on several occcasions in London to discuss Reed's work and the early *B.O.P.*, gave the first eight titles in order of writing as: *The Adventures of a Three-Guinea Watch*, *The Fifth Form at St Dominic's*, *The Master of the Shell*, *My Friend Smith*, *The Willoughby Captains*, *Reginald Cruden*, *Follow My Leader* and *A Dog with a Bad Name*.

Most of Reed's long serial stories were published by the Society in book form or subleased by them for publication by other publishers; the Society no doubt found this welcome source of income a notable bonus in the annual accounts. It seems incredible today that Reed could have been so indifferent to the income from his work as a professional writer of considerable skill. An avid book collector, he seems to have spent his earnings on first editions, special bindings and reference books for his *History of the Old English Letter Foundries*. 'Never did any man more enjoy work for its own sake,' wrote Stanley Morison. 'It is obvious that Reed would have written for no reward whatever. The demand for the product of his pen was more exciting than any payment for it. He was as indifferent to pay for the *B.O.P.* as for the *Earlsmead Chronicle*.' Reed regarded his work for *B.O.P.* as personal service to the cause of Christian literature and the Society. No doubt he shared in the success of the family business, and also received fees for his work on the *Leeds Mercury*, but his *B.O.P.* work was done for the sheer love of the task, and his copyrights in the *B.O.P.* stories were transferred to the Society for little more than token payments.

The Christian, manly and natural tone of Reed's writing seemed far more appropriate to his readers than the larded approach of Dean Farrar in *Eric; or, Little by Little*, a story which fell flat as a pancake among the very boys it was meant to influence (Reed criticised the Dean, and similar writers, in his *Leeds Mercury* articles). The direct, active Christianity advocated in Reed's *B.O.P.* stories had far greater appeal for boys of all social classes, and the type of character he depicted as admirable was

Far right: an illustration by Alfred Pearse from Talbot Baines Reed's school serial, The Willoughby Captains, *which opened on October 6, 1883 and ran until June 7, 1884 (Volume VI). Who was to be the new captain of Willoughby, successor to the splendid Wyndham who was not merely 'head classic' but facile princeps in all the manly sports for which the school was famed? Riddell, the new 'head classic', had only been at Willoughby for two years; he was clumsy on the playing-field, diffident in his manner, had few friends and no gift for leadership, and was even reputed to be 'pi'. Moreover, he shrank from any idea of taking on the captaincy. But the Doctor quietly insisted that he must accept it and stick to it, even when the monitors got up a petition against him (the Doctor returned it unread) and made their own choice of captain, the dashing and athletic Bloomfield*

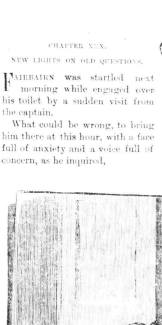

The Willoughby Captains.

A School Story—By

TALBOT BAINES REED.

FAIRBAIRN was startled next morning while engaged over his toilet by a sudden visit from the captain.

What could be wrong, to bring him there at this hour, with a face full of anxiety and a voice full of concern, as he inquired,

"In due time the preliminaries were all got through."

"What *are* you talking about, Riddell," asked Fairbairn, in tones almost of pity. "Has anything happened to you?"

Riddell looked at the speaker inquisitively for a moment, then broke out into a laugh.

"What an ass I am! I forgot to tell you what I wanted them for. The fact is, I asked two kids to breakfast this morning, and I just remembered I had nothing but tea and toast to offer them—and it's too early to get anything in. I'd be awfully obliged if you could help me out with it."

Fairbairn's merriment broke out afresh as the truth revealed itself, and it was some time before he could attend to business. He then offered Riddell anything he could find in his cupboard, and the captain thereupon gratefully availed himself of the offer to secure a pot of red-currant jam, a small jar of potted meat, two or three apples, and a considerable section of a plum cake. All these he promised to replace without delay, and triumphantly hurried back with them in his pockets and under his jacket, in time to deposit them

"Will you do me a favour, old man?"

Fairbairn knew his friend had been in trouble for some time past, and was sore beset on many hands. He had not attempted to intrude into his secrets or to volunteer any aid. For he knew Riddell would ask it if he wanted it. In proof of which here he was.

"Of course I will," replied he, "if I can."

"Do you happen to have a pot of jam you could lend me?"

Fairbairn fairly staggered at this unexpected request. He had imagined he was to be asked at the very least to accompany his friend on some matter of moment to the Doctor's study, or to share some tremendous secret affecting the honour of

Willoughby. And to be asked now for the loan of a pot of jam was too great a shock for his gravity, and he burst out laughing.

"A pot of jam!" he exclaimed. "Whatever do you mean?"

"Oh, any sort you've got," said the captain, eagerly; "and I suppose you haven't got a pie of any kind, or some muffins?"

Fairbairn gaped at his visitor with something like apprehension as he came out with this extraordinary request. The captain's voice was grave and no suspicion of a jest lurked in his face. Could he possibly have succumbed to the mental strain of the past term and taken leave of his wits?

accepted as such by his readers without question. His relative youth, lively enquiring mind, and love of team games, all stood him in good stead. The fact that he was an excellent player at Rugby football, a good cricketer, skilled at all water games and at swimming, won him his readers' immediate respect; and respect was what he, in his turn, felt for them. Reed was one of the first to see the importance of practical education. He wanted to show his readers how to do things really well, in the easy, almost nonchalant, manner which came naturally to him. There was nothing of the sergeant major about Reed, no laying down of the law in tones which boys inevitably resented. 'Look,' Reed said persuasively, 'this is the way to do it! It's quite easy. Practise it until you get it right. Then go on practising—more and more practice—always polish up your personal skill.'

Whatever the themes of his own stories, Reed was concerned that B.O.P.'s appeal should not be restricted to readers from comfortable 'boarding-school' backgrounds. 'The problem for future writers of juvenile literature,' he said, replying to Edward Salmon's criticism in *Juvenile Literature as It Is* that B.O.P. was no more than a substitute for Jack Sheppard and Sweeney Todd, 'is surely to attempt in some bold, effective and practical way to cut into the fields of low literature and give our street boys and girls as good stories as are already provided for the boys and girls of our more happy homes.' I faced much the same problem myself as Editor of B.O.P. in later years, but felt we must be on the right tracks when one day's mail produced letters from boys at public, secondary and grammar schools, boys from country villages, market towns and industrial cities—among them well-written letters from parts of Greater Manchester which I well knew were slum areas. I am sure that Hutchison and Reed realised, as I did, that B.O.P. could appeal to all boys regardless of their upbringing, education or social background.

Reed's philosophy may be summed up by a congratulatory message he sent to a Boys' Club in Manchester on its foundation. Addressing the boys as 'my dear fellows', always a favourite expression of his, he went on to say: 'The strong fellows should look after the weak, the active must look after the lazy, the merry must cheer up the dull, the sharp must lend a helping hand to the duffer. Pull together in all your learning, playing and praying.' Particularly characteristic is the emphasis on cheerfulness. Reed tried hard to instil through B.O.P. his belief in laughter as an essential part of the Christian way of life: boys with a sense of humour and fun could inspire their fellows through their ordinary, everyday lives.

Sir Charles Reed died unexpectedly in 1881, aged sixty-two. Within a short time 'Tibbie' Reed was Managing Director of the Foundry. He had also inherited many voluntary and philanthropic duties of a family nature, first undertaken by his father and his grandfather. In 1884 a further blow was the death at thirty-nine of his eldest brother, the Rev. Charles Reed, who had given much help and advice to 'Tibbie' on B.O.P. matters.

'Tibbie' Reed's commitments were thus considerable, but he never knew when to say 'Enough is enough.' By his fortieth birthday in 1892 it was clear that Reed was grossly overworking. In January 1893 he was forced to tell his friends what his family already knew, that his health was breaking down under the strain and that he was going to Northern Ireland, which he loved so much, for a few months' rest to recuperate. He came back to England in May but was taken seriously ill a month later, and returned to Ireland. His illness was 'consumption', as pulmonary tuberculosis was then known; he was confined to his room but could at least write with much of his old zest. His strength began to fail rapidly and he was brought home again to London, where he died at his home in Highgate on November 28, 1893, aged forty-one. His last work was an article, anonymous as usual, published in the *Leeds Mercury* ten days before his death. He was buried alongside his father and grandfather at the Abney Park Cemetery, and his grave was visited by countless boys and their families for a great many years afterwards.

Whenever the Victorian *B.O.P.* is mentioned, the conversation will turn to the Adventures of a Three-Guinea Watch or Tom, Dick and Harry, to the Cock House at Fellsgarth or the Fifth Form at St Dominic's, to the achievements of Parkhurst on sporting fields, and yarns about a friend named Smith, to a 'dog with a bad name', the Master of the Shell, young Roger Ingleton Minor, the Willoughby Captains ... and 'others too numerous to mention', as Reed would say with infectious good humour. The serials are his true memorial.

The issue of March 19, 1881, included an interesting comment from Hutchison in answer to some early criticism of *B.O.P.* fiction. The first story complained of, *My Doggie and I* by R. M. Ballantyne, ran from December 4, 1880, to March 12, 1881. Its narrator, John Mellon, is a medical student who rescues a shaggy dog, Dumps, from a bullying ruffian. Mellon is a district visitor in Whitechapel and on one of his visits to a widow, Mrs Willis (born a lady, but reduced to abject poverty), he meets an urchin, Slidder, who recognises the dog and says that he had found Dumps as an abandoned pup, cared for him, and eventually sold him to a pretty young lady. Mellon works earnestly to convert Slidder— a cheerful rogue, ready and willing to steal food to keep Mrs Willis alive, and astonished to be told this is wrong—and to comfort the old lady, whose great grief is the disappearance of her only relative, a granddaughter, lovely as a sunbeam, who went out for a walk in the Whitechapel alleys one afternoon, and never returned. Dumps's first owner is rediscovered working as nursery governess to a doctor's family and Mellon honourably returns the dog to her, just in time for Dumps to interrupt a burglary, in the course of which the doctor's house is burnt to the ground. Mellon rescues the governess Lilly Blythe: and thus wins a place as the doctor's assistant for himself, a place as pageboy for Slidder, kindly charity for Mrs Willis, and eventually, Lilly's heart. Slidder is stubbornly on the trail of the missing granddaughter, abducted with her pet dog by the same ruffianly burglar, and concussed in her attempt to escape. She is, of course, revealed as Lilly Blythe, now to become Mellon's bride and to join him and the devoted Slidder in the work of seeking out, caring for, teaching and saving the city's street urchins.

The correspondent who wrote to *B.O.P.* complained, Hutchison said, simply because:

---◆•◆---

A Spiteful Ballad.

In the cupboard I lie, but just close to my eye
There's a very convenient crack in the door;
Through this same I can see how things happen to be,
And can judge who acquaintance with me will deplore.

I can hear " The Head " say, " After fourth school, please stay,"
To some culprit who soon my attentions will need,
And I quiver in spite when I think how I'll bite,
As of sharp castigation I dole out his meed.

I am hated of all, both by great and by small,
And I don't think " The Head " even loves me too well ;
So revenge becomes sweet, and it's really a treat
To tickle a boy up, and tickle him well.

I am supple and tough, and they soon have enough,
Who are doomed for their faults to be touched up by me.
I have plenty of spring, and I know how to sting ;
When at work you should hear how I whistle with glee.

There are some folks who say that long past is my day,
And who call me a relic of barbarous times ;
But that's only a fad, and for boys who are bad
There is nought to convince them so soon of their crimes.

SOMERVILLE GIBNEY.

Above: a set of verses by Somerville Gibney, published on November 12, 1887 (Volume X): a schoolboy relish for 'swishing humour' recurred throughout the Victorian and Edwardian eras and lasted well into the twentieth century

MY DOGGIE AND I.

By R. M. BALLANTYNE,

Author of "The Red Man's Revenge," etc.

CHAPTER V.—CONSPIRACY AND VILLAINY, INNOCENCE
AND TRAGEDY !

IN one of the dirtiest of the dirty and disreputable dens of London a man and a boy sat on that same dark December night, engaged in earnest conversation.

Their seats were stools, their table was an empty flour-barrel, their apartment a cellar. A farthing candle stood awry in the neck of a pint bottle. A broken-lipped jug of gin-and-water hot, and two cracked teacups, stood between them. The damp of the place was drawn out rather than abated by a small fire, which burned in a rusty grate, over which they sought to warm their hands as they conversed. The man was palpably a scoundrel. Not less so was the boy.

Above: one of the illustrations by Walter F. Allen to Ballantyne's My Doggie and I, *published on January 8, 1881 (Volume III); a correspondent complained that no respectable magazine would publish such a tale*

There were some 'rough characters' in it, and also to condemn the illustrations [by Walter F. Allen] for making a burglar look like one (which of course was the precise object of the artist, unless he had deliberately sacrificed truth as well as common-sense, and thus stultified the noble lessons it was the design of the story to teach). We forwarded the complaint to Mr. Ballantyne, who writes: 'It grieves me deeply to find that "My Doggie", which I had earnestly hoped would do good, has given offence in some quarters. One of my chief aims in the story is to show the blessed influence of love, in drawing light, careless, and depraved hearts away from sin towards Jesus, the Saviour from sin. In attempting this I have had to contrast coarse, vulgar, and bad characters with those that are good, tender, and true. Surely the most sensitive of your readers must admit that it is impossible to exhibit such a contrast without a faithful portraiture of both characters. A villain must of necessity speak, look, and act as a villain, if he is to appear on the stage at all!'

By the same post came a letter extolling the Ballantyne story, but complaining about Reed's *Adventures of a Three-Guinea Watch*, on exactly the same grounds. 'The author of the *Watch*,' Hutchison replied, 'is the son of Sir Charles Reed, Chairman of the London School Board', and he quoted Reed's own reply: 'The great strength of the *B.O.P.* (which is far away the healthiest and manliest I know) seems to me to lie in its high moral and religious tone.' 'The *B.O.P.*,' wrote Hutchison, 'esteems far above all other honours that of being a truly Christian paper—helpful in the very highest and best and manliest sense of the word.'

While he was about it, Hutchison rebuked another periodical, *The Christian*, which had criticised *B.O.P.* for publishing any fiction at all. Remarking that Bunyan and Milton, Cowper and Spenser, had all turned fiction to high moral purpose, he went on, 'To determine to issue no such "fiction" would be inevitably to hand over our boys to the tender mercies of the unscrupulous or the actually vicious, who have hitherto but too successfully catered for them.'

The readership supported him. Within the first four years, *B.O.P.* was being used as a school reader—a welcome change from the type of popular reading matter usually allowed in school time. It was 'so well thought of in high places' that Volume IV, 1881-2, was dedicated by special permission to two of its keenest readers, Prince Edward and Prince George of Wales, later to be, respectively, the Duke of Clarence and King George the Fifth. Among the delights of that volume was *The Fifth Form at St Dominic's*.

Above: an extract from the correspondence columns of September 17, 1881 (Volume III), in which subscribers sprang to Hutchison's defence over the use of fiction in B.O.P.

Left: an endpiece from the close of Volume XXXIII (1910-11)

Chapter Four

Quicquid Agunt Pueri Nostri

Above: a line decoration by H. F. Hobden from the first of a series of articles on Yacht, Canoe and Boat-Building *by C. Stansfeld-Hicks, published on July 15, 1882 (Volume IV)*

Far right: articles on boat-building appeared in B.O.P. year after year; this particular one, by D. F. McLachlan, was published on May 20, 1905 (Volume XXVII)

Despite the high quality of the fiction, I have always felt that a great part of *B.O.P.*'s appeal lay in the miscellaneous articles and features, which were of high quality and wide range, and I was interested to see that Gordon felt the same. 'The *Boy's Own* characteristic merit lay in its miscellaneous matter, which was of a much wider range than had been attempted before,' wrote Gordon. 'The best was wanted, put in a readable, interesting way by those who knew, and the practical and constructional articles were by men who had really done what they described, and in most instances brought the models or working drawings or collections with the manuscripts.' Because of this, *B.O.P.* gained an enviable reputation for reliability.

Occasional mistakes were bound to occur, but they were never of a serious nature. In *B.O.P.*'s first forty or fifty years the most vigilant adult critics were schoolmasters. The slightest spelling error, for instance, would draw a shoal of letters. Correspondents sometimes wrote to *B.O.P.* months, even years, after a slip had occurred, evidence of the way readers continued to refer to back numbers. Clergymen often rivalled schoolmasters in their rebukes. The readers only complained about the number of pages . . . they simply wanted more magazine for their penny!

How-to-make-it material, full plans and diagrams, and the most detailed hints for making a success of any project, were of major importance from the start. The second number featured the remarkable traveller John MacGregor (1825–92). 'Rob Roy' MacGregor launched his first canoe in 1865 and paddled it down the rivers and across the lakes of Europe, covering a thousand miles in three months. The log of this first voyage, published in 1866, went through thirteen editions in under twenty years, and his infectious enthusiasm for the sport is said to have introduced canoeing into Britain. MacGregor's breezy, spirited descriptions for *B.O.P.* of voyages by canoe and yawl became deservedly popular. 'Nearing the lighthouse off Dungeness,' he wrote in an account of one cross-Channel trip, 'I came into the tide which was running at high speed and in dancing waves so upright and sharp that there was not room between

THE BOY'S OWN

SAILING SKIFF

AND HOW TO BUILD IT

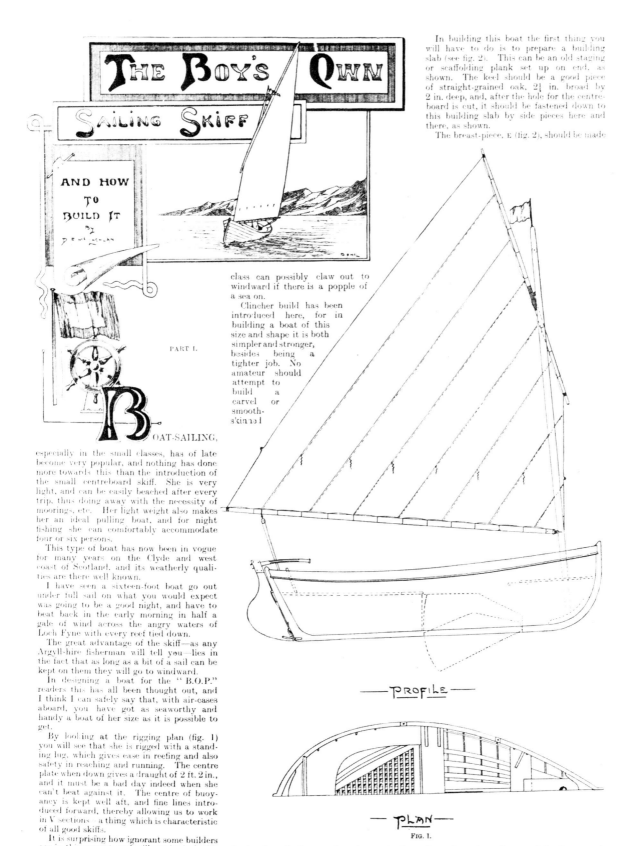

PART I.

BOAT-SAILING, especially in the small classes, has of late become very popular, and nothing has done more towards this than the introduction of the small centreboard skiff. She is very light, and can be easily beached after every trip, thus doing away with the necessity of moorings, etc. Her light weight also makes her an ideal pulling boat, and for night fishing she can comfortably accommodate four or six persons.

This type of boat has now been in vogue for many years on the Clyde and west coast of Scotland, and its weatherly qualities are there well known.

I have seen a sixteen-foot boat go out under full sail on what you would expect was going to be a good night, and have to beat back in the early morning in half a gale of wind across the angry waters of Loch Fyne with every reef tied down.

The great advantage of the skiff—as any Argyll-hire fisherman will tell you—lies in the fact that as long as a bit of a sail can be kept on them they will go to windward.

In designing a boat for the "B.O.P." readers this has all been thought out, and I think I can safely say that, with air-cases aboard, you have got as seaworthy and handy a boat of her size as it is possible to get.

By looking at the rigging plan (fig. 1) you will see that she is rigged with a standing lug, which gives ease in reefing and also safety in reaching and running. The centre plate when down gives a draught of 2 ft. 2 in., and it must be a bad day indeed when she can't beat against it. The centre of buoyancy is kept well aft, and fine lines introduced forward, thereby allowing us to work in V sections—a thing which is characteristic of all good skiffs.

It is surprising how ignorant some builders are in this respect, and will persist in building their boats with round sections forward, for it stands to reason that no boat of that

class can possibly claw out to windward if there is a popple of a sea on.

Clincher build has been introduced here, for in building a boat of this size and shape it is both simpler and stronger, besides being a tighter job. No amateur should attempt to build a carvel or smooth-skinned

boat unless she is over three beams to the length, or her planking exceeds $\frac{5}{8}$ in., as there is no getting her watertight.

In building this boat the first thing you will have to do is to prepare a building slab (see fig. 2). This can be an old staging or scaffolding plank set up on end, as shown. The keel should be a good piece of straight-grained oak, $2\frac{1}{4}$ in. broad by 2 in. deep, and, after the hole for the centreboard is cut, it should be fastened down to this building slab by side pieces here and there, as shown.

The breast-piece, E (fig. 2), should be made

from dimensions given, and firmly screwed down to this keel, as shown, using brass screws, of course, for you must remember

— PROFILE —

— PLAN —

FIG. 1.

REV. T. M. MILLINGTON.

MR. PAUL BLAKE.

them for the yawl to dip over one and then to rise on the next.' In these stormy seas his dinghy broke her tow—'Down with the helm—haul the sheet—splash, dash, spray-flakes and wave-foam—chase her, catch her, heave her on board, the saucy truant—and then loud applauding hurrahs came from the lighthouse-men in their eyrie aloft' (October 4, 1879). An active and committed Christian, a member of the London School Board, and a man of vigorous outdoor interests, MacGregor was an excellent choice to begin *B.O.P.*'s long career of instructing and encouraging youthful boat-builders and would-be seamen. A week later, on February 1, 1879, appeared *My Boat and How I Made It*; it was to be the first of many such articles. In one year of the magazine's existence, 1879–80, readers learned how to build a 12-foot boat, *Swallow*; a serviceable ice-boat; a sturdy punt; and a whole fleet of model ships. (W. Herbert Holloway, a *B.O.P.* contributor for many years—the type of man the magazine attracted and held like a magnet—was particularly known for his detailed and meticulous drawings of all kinds and types of boats; twenty of his models of African boats and canoes are still at the Science Museum in London.) Along the way there were articles on knots and cordage, how to net and sling a hammock, how to rig a flagstaff, and allied matters. Seventy-five years later, in my own time as Editor, we counted among our regular contributors Percy Blandford, a world authority on sailing, canoeing and aquatic adventure.

The enterprise and courage of 'Rob Roy' MacGregor and others like him brightened the early issues of *B.O.P.* An article in the eighth issue by Thomas Baines, artist and African explorer (1822–75) and one-time colleague of Livingstone, set the pattern for a long connection with missionaries in far-distant places, explorers, big-game hunters, men of adventure living in remote, dangerous, deserted corners of the world. The Religious Tract Society had a trump card here. First-hand accounts of life in the mission field made splendid reading for boys everywhere, but Hutchison's many contacts were not confined to men of the Society. He developed the idea of 'special correspondents', men engaged on hazardous duties in places where danger always threatened—lonely forests, tropical jungles and river valleys, low-lying swamps or mountain passes. David Ker was the first of many such Special Correspondents to make their mark in *B.O.P.* He wrote his despatches in jet-black ink in the tiniest, but perfectly legible, script on very thin sheets of notepaper, folded into strips that fitted snugly into his revolver case, so that he could pack a story or despatch of more than a dozen chapters into less than five cubic inches. *B.O.P.* was very proud of David Ker who soon had a wide following.

Among the other early successes was *Battles with the Sea* (1881), a long series of lifeboat articles by R. M. Ballantyne, which Hutchison planned and inspired. Hutchison suggested that readers who had been stirred by this series should collect funds to launch the *Boy's Own Lifeboat*; when they seemed dilatory he urged them on ('No reader of the *B.O.P.* should fail to send us something, however small'). Two RNLI boats were eventually launched as a result of *B.O.P.* appeals, which raised over £1,200; readers loved to read accounts of thrilling real-life rescues in which their *own* lifeboats took part.

A Day out with a Bicycle Club.

1. On the way to the rendezvous : Obstructives.
5. The March Past.
2. Bicyclist (loq.) "Good-bye, old fellow, I can't wait."
3. Coming down hill. "Facile descensus."
4. Our Bugler : an object of intense admiration.

Outdoor games and healthy open-air interests were always well to the fore. The dividing line between lively fiction, lightly disguising its instructive nature, and adventurous fact, was never very strong, particularly in the Victorian *B.O.P.*; stories and features alike stressed the open-air theme, encouraging readers to get out and about whenever possible. A stalwart supporter and Committee member, the Rev. T. S. Millington, who had begun his long connection with *B.O.P.* in February, 1879, contributed a typical short serial, *Our Holiday Tramp* in the summer of 1880. A baker's dozen of cheerful schoolboys explored the local countryside in the summer holidays and learnt a great many lessons in the process. The following summer, on July 9, 1881, appeared the first in a series of articles by the versatile writer, Paul Blake (pen-name of H. M. Paull) who contributed fiction, non-fiction and verse to *B.O.P.* for many years. His description of a boating trip from Oxford to Richmond, *A Week on the Thames*, sent *B.O.P.* readers out in droves and was said to have done

Above and below: cycling was featured in B.O.P. from penny-farthing days (March 6, 1880), via Bywayman's strenuous tours (March, 1938), to the post-war era (when Ronald English became the resident cycle expert)

ON PAINTING IN WATER COLOUR.

BY HUME NISBET,

Author of "A Plain Guide to Oil Painting," etc. etc.

(With Illustrations by various Representative "Boy's Own" Artists.)

A Sketch. for the B.O.P

Above: one of a series for the amateur artist, this item appeared in B.O.P. on February 13, 1897 (Volume XIX). Just a year earlier the paper had published the same author's Plain Guide to Oil Painting *(from July 18 to September 19, 1896; Volume XVIII). Among its readers was a Scottish lad, James McBey, living in the bleak windswept countryside of Buchan, Aberdeenshire. McBey read the articles so often that he could virtually repeat them word for word. They instilled in him the hope that he might one day be able to make his living as a painter. For fourteen years, in the best B.O.P. tradition, he studied and practised until, at the age of twenty-six, he was able to discard his safe job in a bank and devote himself to an artistic career that was to bring him distinction and fame. His autobiography recorded the debt he felt he owed to B.O.P.*

as much for the old river as Scott's *The Lady of the Lake* had done for the Trossachs.

The issue of April 24, 1880, to choose an example almost at random, was made up as follows:

(a) episodes from two long-running serials (Verne's *The Boy Captain* and Kingston's *Peter Trawl*) and the second part of a two-part story (*A Narrow Escape*, by 'An Old Soldier')

(b) an article on life in the Merchant Navy ('We have never known a well-behaved, honest-looking youngster fail in obtaining a berth within a week')

(c) *Boys' Dogs and All About Them*, by Dr William Gordon Stables, a classic B.O.P. contributor whose work is described more fully in Chapter 5

(d) a religious anecdote complete with hymn

(e) one of an illustrated series of articles on *Bicycles and Bicycling*, an activity featured in *B.O.P.* throughout its history (Ronald English was the cycling expert in my own time as Editor)

(f) *Bees and Bee-Keeping for Boys* ('wonderful, interesting and profitable insects')

(g) one of a series of features on solitaire, a game which, with draughts and chess, was given particularly good coverage in the early years (H. F. L. Meyer's chess articles began in February 1879 and were still running, fresh as paint, 35 years later)

(h) *Birds' Eggs and Egg-Collecting* by the Rev. J. G. Wood—perhaps this was one of the articles he wrote in the train, on his way to Paternoster Row? Wood owned a portable typewriter, an invention then in its infancy, and on at least one occasion his fellow passengers were astonished to see this clerical author tapping away at the strange machine which was perched on the seat beside him

(i) lastly, supplanting the usual correspondence column, *Useful Employments for Spare Hours*—in this case, building rustic garden furniture.

Alongside outdoor sports went indoor amusements, particularly of a scientific kind. The chemist Dr Scoffern joined *B.O.P.*'s contributors in August, 1880, with features on glass-blowing for boys ('the beginning of all practical chemistry') and how to make a shower of fire, using sugar of lead (readers who inadvertently swallowed any of this poisonous substance were advised to take a good dose of Epsom salts). Chemical experiments, 'scientific odds and ends', the study of electricity, and so on, led naturally to optical tricks and conjuring. Among the early contributors to *B.O.P.* was John Nevil Maskelyne (1839-1917), famous Victorian conjuror and founder of a theatre of magic which his family ran in London for over fifty years. *Ghosts at Holly Court*, by a 'Genuine Medium' which appeared in Volume II, was an exposé of tricks practised by the unscrupulous. But *B.O.P.*'s staff was ready and willing to enjoy a good ghost story—'all the more if it makes the blood curdle and blanches the cheek'—and the outstanding capture of the early years was yet another doctor of medicine in the person of Arthur Conan Doyle, MD, said to have set the Christmas issue for 1883 afire with *My Lecture on Dynamite*.

Nothing is now known of how the twenty-four-year-old Conan Doyle (1859-1930) first came to contribute to *B.O.P.* Perhaps, like Stables, he was introduced by Macaulay, now nearly seventy, and acting as *B.O.P.*'s father figure, with his snug skull-cap, flowing majestic beard, and air of genuine antiquity. On the occasion of the magazine's twenty-fifth birthday, Conan Doyle wrote a note of congratulations remarking that *B.O.P.* 'was one of the first papers which grew tired of returning my mss, and began to print them instead'. *My Lecture on Dynamite* went down so well that he followed it with *The Fate of the Evangeline*, Christmas 1884, and *An Exciting Christmas Eve* for 1885. A year later Hutchison published Conan Doyle's serial story, *Uncle Jeremy's Household*. It became a *B.O.P.* classic. Written in the chilling manner beloved of boys, Conan Doyle's stories could be read aloud to the family circle, with all lights extinguished save one shaded candle. As the story unfolded, the listeners huddled closer and closer to one another, and at the critical moment the narrator snuffed the candle, plunging the room into total blackness, while a partner in crime opened a window to introduce the necessary icy draught, and another contrived owl hoots, mysterious moans, or peals of maniacal laughter.

SOME STRAIGHTFORWARD CONJURING TRICKS.

DESCRIBED BY DR. SCOFFERN.

PHARAOH'S SERPENTS.

FROM time to time more than one young gentleman has addressed the Editor, soliciting information about the so-called "Pharaoh's Serpents" — what they were made of, whether young fellows could make them—or, rather, make the stuff of which they were made —whether dangerous to

make, dangerous to burn in a room, and so on. Further, one young gentleman made a most pathetic appeal—enough almost, I should say, to thaw the heart of any editor, frozen hard to appeals generally as editorial hearts are wont to be. Well, the matter has been deliberately thought over—the *pros* and *cons* of danger or no danger have been considered, and with the result that I shall presently describe the manufacture of the serpents' eggs, from which, when set alight, come the serpents.

Folks, old as well as young, who go dabbling in chemical manufacture, are all subject to one and the same drawback (if you choose to look upon it as a drawback), and it is this. Very frequently, in order to make the thing they wish to make, they must make the thing or things to make it with. Take the present case. Pharaoh's serpents' eggs are made from *sulpho-cyanide of mercury*. Sulpho-cyanide of mercury results from the mixture of sulpho-cyanide of potassium with nitrate of mercury, to make which you must previously have made both these compounds.

However, let us begin. Provide yourself with an iron ladle, some sulphur, some yellow prussiate of potash—known to chemists as "ferro-cyanide of potassium" — quicksilver, nitric acid—the shop-name of which is aqua-fortis—filtering-paper, a funnel, gum-water, a little nitre, and a bottle of distilled water. You must have—or at least you *ought* to have—in addition a Wedgwood mortar. An ingenious young fellow could do without a mortar, by crushing or rolling ; he must, however, by no means lay the cook's rolling-pin under contribution !

Above: this article appeared on April 9, 1881 (Volume III). 'Yellow prussiate of potash,' said the good doctor sturdily, 'is no more poisonous than Epsom salts'—though readers might find it hard to convince their local druggist of the fact

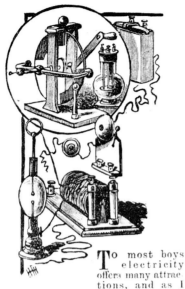

To most boys electricity offers many attractions, and as I have recently constructed an induction coil out of materials which are cheap and easily obtained, I think I shall confer a benefit on many readers of the B.O.P. if I give them a short description of how this was accomplished, so that if like-minded they can proceed in the same way. Induction coils may be used for medical and scientific purposes as well as for amusement, so that a good deal of work comes within their scope. An "induction coil" is composed principally of two portions—one is the "primary" coil, the other the "secondary." It is the secondary coil that gives the spark, and on the length of this depends the power of the coil ; in some instruments for scientific purposes it is composed of a wire nearly 300 *miles* long—but we are not going to soar to such heights as that !

To make the coil itself you will want an ounce of "No. 24" cotton-covered wire, and two or three ounces of "No. 36." This can be bought from an ironmonger who deals in such materials, or there are special shops for the purpose, such as Dale's of Ludgate Hill. If you are very ambitious, silk-covered wire can be used; this gives

Above: How to Make an Induction Coil, *one of the first of R. A. R. Bennett's contributions to B.O.P., published on April 6, 1889 (Volume XI)*

Uncle Jeremy's Household was a great success with house parties. It ran from January 8 to February 19, 1887, and was beautifully illustrated with original wood-engravings by Richard Caton Woodville, RA. I reprinted Chapter VI in *B.O.P.*'s seventy-fifth birthday number, in March 1954, and received a delightful letter from a new reader, Anthony Caton Woodville of Dawlish, Devon, who wrote: 'When I bought my first copy of *B.O.P.*, the seventy-fifth Birthday Number, March 1954, I was most surprised to see an illustration in it by my great-grandfather, Richard Caton Woodville, with Conan Doyle's *Uncle Jeremy's Household*. He did the work 67 years ago.' This constant linking of past and present always seemed to be a feature of *B.O.P.*

Hutchison and Gordon believed strongly in the importance of contemporary advances in mechanical engineering, and encouraged their readers to share something of the satisfaction to be found in practical project work. H. F. Hobden, for instance, who joined *B.O.P.*'s contributors in 1884, wrote a series of illustrated articles on building a model launch engine—'a perfect model of an inverted-cylinder direct-action engine with link-motion reversing gear'. A few weeks later, on January 24, 1885, *B.O.P.* published an article on the flight of Tissandier's airship, which had taken place over Paris four months earlier. 'We chronicle its success as being one more step towards the long-hoped-for solution of that great problem of these later days, the navigation of the atmosphere.' Here again, fiction played its part. Alongside tales of school life (*Peter's Perplexities in Pursuit of Science; The Heroes of New Swishford; Our Cricket Match at Sandilands;* etc.) and adventures overseas (*The Star of the South—a Tale of the Diamond Fields; The Prairie Chief; Ilderim the Afghan*) were serials buoyant with belief in scientific advance. In 1886 readers revelled in the sheer brilliance of Verne's *The Clipper of the Clouds*, and two years later Verne and Grousset collaborated as 'André Laurie' in *A Marvellous Conquest*—the conquered territory being the moon.

None the less, pre-eminent throughout *B.O.P.*'s first decade was the theme struck in the opening issues: that of the sea. Articles on boat-building, sailing, canoeing, etc., and breezy adventure stories (*Up and Down—a Tale of the Ocean Wave; Homeward Bound—a True Tale of the Sea; On Special Service—a Naval Story*) were supplemented by features on careers afloat. In Volume XII, 1889-90, for instance, was a series of five long articles★, illustrated by the author, depicting life on board *Britannia*, the floating forerunner of the present Britannia Royal Naval College. Written by Captain F. C. D. Bedford, RN, CB, they appeared between June 7 and July 5, 1890; the vivid descriptive writing and the clarity of the drawings bore clearly the mark of firsthand knowledge, hardly surprising since Captain Bedford had been in command of *Britannia* from 1886-9. They provide a fascinating account of life for naval cadets on the River Dart in the halcyon days of 1890, before the present College was built on the famous hill above the Devon river.

In the same volume appeared the first of a long run of how-to-make-it and what-to-do-next articles by R. A. R. Bennett. *How To Make a*

★ Reproduced in the *Britannia Magazine*, 1979, Summer Number, as part of the Royal Naval College's seventy-fifth birthday celebrations.

The Boy's Own Model Gas Engine

AND HOW TO MAKE IT.

by - H.F. Hobden

Author of the "Boy's Own Windmill," "Model Launch Engine," etc. etc.

PART I.

SMALL-POWER engine that can be quickly started, and with no troublesome boiler to be constantly seen to or any skilled attendant required, but which can be easily kept in proper order by any one of the family, will be found of constant use for such purposes as driving the various domestic machines that now have a place in almost every home.

Judging from the numerous inquiries for such a machine, there is evidently a genuine want, and to supply this I propose showing in as short a manner as possible how you may construct a small gas engine for yourselves, at a moderate cost for materials, which will drive a sewing machine, or a fan for ventilating, keep a pump going to supply a fountain or aquarium, or do any of the hundred and one little jobs that such a small motor is equal to.

Gas is now in such general use that, except in very out-of-the-way districts, there is no difficulty about the supply; but in case any of my readers should be dwelling in some country place, or in a house which is not supplied with gas, I will explain later on how he may generate gas for himself by means of a very simple contrivance known as a vaporiser.

There are several reasons why the size of our engine should not exceed the dimensions I have fixed on. First, because of the

Condenser for an Induction Coil had appeared earlier, anonymously; now he taught his readers how to make a 'simple electrical machine', an electric lamp, an electromotor, etc., and how to carry out some simple electrical experiments. (The magic of electricity and the joys of life at sea were agreeably combined in the same volume in *The Wire and the Wave*, a lively story by J. Monro, with an ingenuous young hero who sees an advertisement for a trainee electrician, applies without knowing what an electrician *is*—neither his parents nor his dictionary can help—and finds himself cable-laying in the Coral Sea.) Readers held Mr Bennett in awe.

Above: H. F. Hobden's articles, written and illustrated by himself, instructed boys in the mysteries of making anything and everything from a model fire escape to a full-size rowing-punt; the gas engine feature appeared on February 9, 1895 (Volume XVII)

What he said must be right. He was an enthusiast for another popular hobby, photography, and founded the *Boy's Own Postal Photographic Club*, with Hutchison's willing support.

B.O.P. encouraged its readers to turn every spare moment to advantage, and Hutchison and Gordon were always in search of fillers for the games and hobbies pages. Team games for the holidays were particularly in demand, for this was an era of large families and social gatherings. Sunday schools and choirs made Bank Holiday trips by special train to the seaside for a breath of salty air. Aunts, uncles and innumerable cousins gathered for family Christmases, complete with party games. Such articles as *How To Be A Clairvoyant at Your Christmas Party*, with instructions so detailed that no one could go wrong, proved a huge success. Music and songs appeared at regular intervals. Some were stirring songs of patriotic origin for the parish concert; others were light, amusing melodies for an evening round the piano in the parlour.

Among the contributors were young officers only too glad to supplement their modest allowances as long as their articles could be published anonymously. One of those who supplied 'miscellaneous' material and fillers was a lieutenant from a crack cavalry regiment, the 13th Hussars: R. S. S. Baden-Powell. Red-haired and freckled, popular with all who came into contact with him, this eager and impecunious young man was twenty-two when B.O.P. was founded, and had just completed two years' duty as a subaltern in India. In 1881 a minor shooting accident left him with a bullet in his left heel. He spent his convalescence improving his languages and writing articles illustrated with his own sketches. These articles he sent off to the *Graphic* in London whose editor took the lot and paid him a guinea each for them. From that time onwards he wasted no time. His daily diary included notes of anything which might come in useful for articles and short stories; and he soon became a B.O.P. contributor. His work was strictly anonymous, but it is not difficult to spot his characteristic style in articles which are written with strict attention to detail and a pleasant touch of humour, and illustrated with his own drawings and sketches.

On his third trip to India, Baden-Powell spent two months bear-hunting in Kashmir, with necessary but irksome waits between bursts of action. In the pauses he jotted down headings for a handbook on Army scouting for cavalry. It was essentially a book of practical advice for young officers, which made use of all the material he found so useful in training his own men: how to track expertly, what deductions to draw from spoor and disturbed trails, the importance of personal hygiene, the value of the daily cold tub at all times of the year, comfort under canvas, careful preparation of food, first aid, signalling of all kinds, and so on.

Baden-Powell was greatly disappointed when W. Thacker & Co., the leading firm of publishers for books on military subjects in India, rejected the manuscript of *Aids to Scouting* on the grounds that sales would be too modest. However, Gale & Polden Ltd, of Aldershot, accepted it at once, offering a royalty of £5 per thousand after the first 2,000 copies had been cleared. Baden-Powell corrected and returned the proofs in October, 1899, by which time he was in South Africa, busy with the defence of Mafeking against the Boers, which was to win him world-wide fame

Sir R. Baden Powell and some of his Boy Scouts.
(*Drawn for the " Boy's Own Paper " by* T. P. BURGESS.)

almost overnight. His little book, *Aids to Scouting*★, achieved lasting success in almost every country of the world. A new patriotic boys' magazine, *Boys of Our Empire*, published by Cassell, serialized it under the intriguing title of *The Boy Scouts*. The sub-editor who prepared it for the press, and chose the excellent title (picked up again in 1908 when the famous Boy Scout movement began), was Arthur Haydon, who was later to succeed Hutchison as *B.O.P.*'s editor.

★   The basis of *Scouting for Boys* which Baden-Powell published in 1908 after running a trial camp for boys at Brownsea Island, Dorset.

The siege of Mafeking lasted 217 days and made Baden-Powell a national hero. Boys at home envied their Mafeking contemporaries whose energies and enthusiasm had been harnessed by Lord Edward Cecil. The Mafeking Cadet Corps, formed by 'Ned' Cecil, wore simple khaki uniforms, and used bicycles as transport; they delivered urgent messages, civilian mail and medical supplies, acted as orderlies, took turns at look-out posts and became an essential part of the Mafeking defences. Baden-Powell arranged for a photograph of the Corps leader, Sgt-Major Warner Goodyear, aged 13, to be used on the official penny stamp. When the siege was at last lifted, on May 17, 1900, the relieving force brought piles of British newspapers for troops and townsfolk, and a bulky parcel addressed to the Cadet Corps, at Baden-Powell's request. It contained twenty copies of every weekly issue of *B.O.P.* the boys had missed. That was Baden-Powell's tribute.

In 1904 Baden-Powell, 'a well-known non-smoker', was chosen as patron of the League of Health and Manliness. He had smoked as a young subaltern but gave it up soon after arriving in India. 'I have altogether given up smoking,' he wrote to his mother, 'it saves a big item in the mess bill.' *B.O.P.* campaigned against smoking, but met with little success. Fathers were all in favour of their sons plunging into cold baths, eating porridge, playing energetic Rugby football and stylish cricket, and so on, but criticism of paternal smoking was a very different matter; and a 'No Smoking' crusade which was loftily disregarded by the adults made little appeal to the older boys who were the bulk of *B.O.P.*'s readership. Moreover, some of *B.O.P.*'s competitors, notably *The Captain*, carried advertisements for Player's Navy Cut cigarettes and showed young men lolling nonchalantly at bamboo tables in the summer sun, smoking cigarettes and drinking liquid refreshment in long glasses. Hutchison could not afford to antagonise parents on the prickly subject of smoking and eventually brought the campaign to a tactful close.

Baden-Powell remained on the most cordial terms with Hutchison and Gordon (whom he rated highly for his vast and accurate knowledge of sports and pastimes, hobbies and 'the interests of real boys') and with Hutchison's successor, Haydon. One of his closest associates, Colonel J. S. Wilson, Camp Chief of the International Scout Leaders Training Centre at Gilwell Park, told me that Baden-Powell never missed reading anything written by 'Tibbie' Reed or Gordon Stables, and much enjoyed the work of David Ker, George Manville Fenn and Arthur Conan Doyle. Baden-Powell's own writings appeared in *B.O.P.* during the First World War, and the link between the magazine and the Scouting movement was always strong. Two later editors, Pocklington and myself, were Scout Commissioners, and many of my contributors were well-known Scout Leaders. None gave greater service to the magazine than my own assistant, Fred Reeve, who had been on the staff of the Scout Association before joining me. A great Assistant Editor if there ever was one. Others included the author, Arthur Catherall; Ronald English, our cycling expert; Percy Blandford; Bill Hillcourt of New Hampshire, USA; and many more.

Chapter Five

The Brine and the Breeze

A renowned *B.O.P.* contributor deserving a chapter to himself was the remarkable Dr Stables. Verne rose to the heights of vivid imaginative fiction, but Stables told 'true-life' adventure, sometimes as factual accounts, sometimes in lightly fictional form. In 1877, two years before *B.O.P.* began, he had published *Jungle, Peak and Plain*; in 1881 it was followed by *Wild Adventures in Wild Places*. Here was the real stuff of adventure in foreign lands, set down in racily readable fashion.

William Gordon Stables was supremely versatile. He contributed fact, fiction, answers to correspondents (highly abrasive), medical advice (he was 'Medicus' of the *Girl's Own Paper* for some thirty years), articles on pets. He was a world authority on dogs, in particular the Newfoundland, his favourite breed, and Verne's own Newfoundland puppy is said to have been a gift from Stables.

His background is fascinating. Descended from a branch of the Gordon clan, he was born in 1840 at Aberchirder in Banffshire, and brought up near Aberdeen. He seemed destined for the church or the army, but instead read medicine at Aberdeen University. While still a student, he took himself off to Arctic waters aboard a whaling brig of 300 tons. The ship was trapped in the ice-pack, and reported lost, and he returned home to find his family in deep mourning. It was no surprise when he joined the Royal Navy as a qualified surgeon. Naval service took him all over the world—to the Mediterranean, East Africa, the Indian Ocean. He had a brilliantly retentive visual memory, as vivid as a reel of film, and this gave his work great authenticity. 'Jungle fever' invalided him out of the Navy on half-pay, after only nine years' service. He married and settled down at Twyford, Berkshire, in a family house which he nicknamed 'The Jungle'. Here he and his wife brought up a family of four sons and two daughters. Faced with the need to provide for his family, Stables turned his expert knowledge of dogs to good use. In the course of his life he was to own over two hundred; in the garden of 'The Jungle' were headstones recording the names and awards of his favourites. He became Kennel Editor of the *Livestock Journal* and was in demand all over the

Above: a line decoration from the title page of the Summer supplement, 1894

DR. GORDON STABLES.

Above: the inimitable Dr Gordon Stables,
1840-1910

country as a show judge. Two of his books, *Our Friend the Dog* and *The Practical Kennel Guide*, are classics of their kind.

Macaulay and Stables had been friends in their medical days. Feeling that his fellow-Scot had something of value to offer to *B.O.P.*, and knowing that Hutchison would never let slip a good story, Macaulay set the ball rolling by making the introductions. Hutchison was fascinated by Stables's stories of his whaling experiences and suggested a *B.O.P.* serial. *The Cruise of the Snowbird* began on March 19, 1881. 'It required *considerable* revision,' wrote Gordon; adding cheerfully, 'but readers knew nothing of that, and *The Cruise of the Snowbird* and its many successors, with their two Scottish heroes, received a hearty welcome, particularly north of the Border.' From that moment on, Gordon became heavily involved with Stables's work: rewriting, revising, cutting, expanding.

Over two hundred Stables features appeared in *B.O.P.* One and all stressed the *B.O.P.* virtues of manliness, courage in the face of danger, whether physical and moral, cheerfulness in adversity, and kindness to others, especially the vulnerable—women and children, elderly people, the crippled, handicapped and destitute. Despite his brusque replies to readers' queries in *B.O.P.* (Chapter 6) he was a kindly man at heart. The brusqueness was probably a direct result of his abrasive early training in the Royal Navy. He could be a delightful companion, full of fun and lively tales. Strong as his prejudices were, his stories were free of the sickening overt emphasis on class which spoiled so much Victorian writing. Whatever a boy's background, whether he wore top hat and tail coat, and strolled across the playing-fields of Eton, or kicked a ball down the London streets in a cloth cap and hand-me-downs, good sportsmanship and a love of the outdoor life were what counted in Stables's opinion. His articles, urging the value of fresh air, regular exercise and cold tubs, probably had an even greater influence on his readers than the tremendous adventure serials, for they gave his remarkable personality its fullest scope.

Mrs Sarah Graham, MA, SRN, whose research into his life and work has occupied many years, describes him as 'an enormously popular figure, with the same sort of fame and influence as the much-loved Uncles of the early BBC *Children's Hour* radio programmes'. He was perhaps too diversified, too eccentric, too much of an individual altogether. But did it matter? 'My *B.O.P.* boys', as he called his readers, meant a great deal to him. His flamboyance, the Highland dress he always wore, the New-foundland dog always at his heel, his sheer personality and character, all were sincere and thus endearing.

A man of many interests, Stables was a pioneer of caravanning in Britain and the first Vice-President of the Caravan Club on its formation in 1907. He personally designed his famous 'land yacht' as he called it, *The Wanderer*, and had it built for him by no less than the Bristol Wagon Company, makers of Pullman cars. This magnificent 30-hundredweight van, preserved for many years at Bristol, has now been restored to its full Victorian glory, with gleaming mahogany and maple, glowing stained glass, and upholstery in chocolate-brown, vermilion, black and gold. Aboard *Wanderer* Stables made his annual pilgrimage across England, from spring to autumn; he played 'the gentleman gipsy' with Foley, his

THE CRUISE OF THE SNOWBIRD.

By GORDON STABLES, M.D., R.N.,

Author of "Jungle, Peak, and Plain," etc., etc.

CHAPTER XXIX.

O N the twentieth day of July, eighteen hundred and ever so much, but just one month from the day they had landed the Yankee trapper in the wild country in which he was monarch of all he surveyed, the brave yacht Snowbird, after many never-to-be-forgotten dangers and trials, had reached the latitude of 81 deg. north, and was far to the east of Spitzbergen. It is a month since we have seen her, and now she is lying-to in front of a tremendous bar of ice, through which she has

The Welcome Home.

personal valet and cook, and Coachman John in charge of the two Suffolk punches, Peaseblossom and Cornflower. His 1896 tour from Twyford to Inverness and back, was a 1,300-mile journey, the *pièce de résistance* of them all. Each year while on the road Stables wrote all his articles and features (his books he reserved for winter work in his 'garden study' at 'The Jungle'). *The Wanderer* was his base but he liked to take off on cycle tours,

Above: an illustration by Gordon Browne from the concluding episode of The Cruise of the Snowbird, *published on September 24, 1881 (Volume III)*

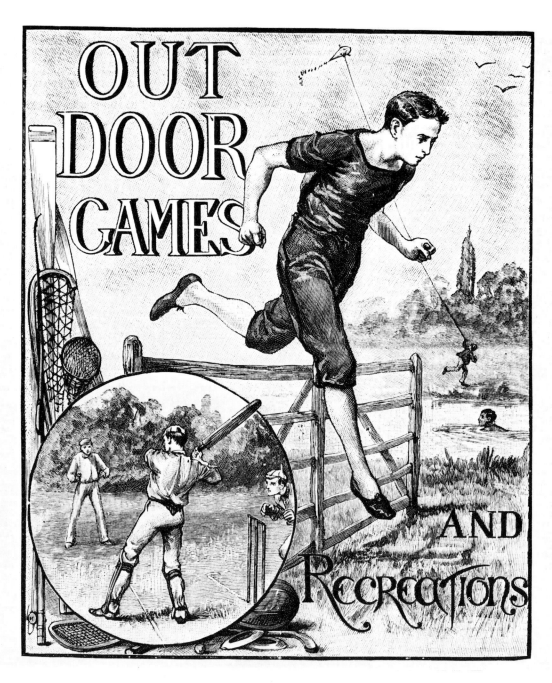

TO BE COMPLETED IN TWELVE MONTHLY PARTS, SIXPENCE EACH.

Edited by G. A. HUTCHISON, Editor "Boy's Own Paper," "Boy's Own Bookshelf," etc., etc.

Above: Outdoor Games and Recreations, *published in twelve monthly parts at sixpence each, appeared in 1891-92. It included articles on cricket by W. G. Grace, swimming by Captain Webb, and many other sports (football, tennis, sailing, skating, fishing, cycling, lacrosse, golf); pastimes such as brass-rubbing, amateur photography and keeping goats; and, of course, 'health hints for growing boys' by Dr Gordon Stables*

or on a favourite tricycle, with the object of gaining copy. The cycling tours filled the long summer evenings, an antidote to long hours of trundling along country roads and lanes in the famous caravan, laden with baggage and gear. Stables never missed a chance of converting his experiences into saleable material as articles or books, and in due course published *Health upon Wheels* and *Rota Vitae*.

Wanderer was fitted with a tram-car brake as well as a powerful iron skid which locked one wheel when descending steep hills. A roller was towed on the chain bridle to check the back wheel 'should the horses stumble while straining uphill and *Wanderer* decide to go hard astern'.

Underneath the caravan were slung buckets, ladders, a spacious tent and a vast collection of miscellaneous hardware. Not an inch of space was wasted; John's driving seat did duty as the corn-bin. Stables took along his harmonium, violin and Spanish guitar, a small piano stool and proper music racks! He also carried a Royal Navy sword and 'a good revolver'. His inevitable Newfoundland dog went too, and so did a grey parrot reminiscent of naval days. The first two weeks on the road were 'rather upsetting, a little like living in a mill'—the jingle-jangle must have been intolerable on Victorian country roads, despite the attempts to deaden it with wedges of softwood, india-rubber, cotton wool and tow. Crowds of curious onlookers gathered wherever *Wanderer* stopped.

The kindness and hospitality of *B.O.P.* and *G.O.P.* readers were very evident on these marvellous summer expeditions. Readers of all ages listened with respect to impromptu wayside lectures, resolving to discard such evil habits as smoking home-made cigarettes or pipes of the cheapest and nastiest strong tobacco, and using snuff 'which your mothers will be sure to find out about since it leaves the ugliest of stains upon lawn handkerchiefs'. All along the route readers provided gifts of food, which considerably reduced the doctor's expenses—fresh eggs and succulent chickens, slices of ham, pigeon squabs ready for the pot, trout fresh from the loch, a steak of Tay salmon with a jug of mayonnaise, home-made wine, pork chops, delicious German sausage for the midday meal with new-baked bread, local butter and tomatoes, fresh-pulled cider and a bag of apples for the journey!

The doctor's staff had a touch of originality about them too. John the Coachman, seen in photographs in a top hat replete with cockade, was very whiskery but always impeccably dressed, a gloved hand holding the head of one of the horses. Valet–Cook–Man-about-the-House Foley was a round-faced youngish man in a bowler hat. He was photographed sitting cross-legged on the ground beside the Ripingilles stove on which he prepared delicious meals, all the better for being eaten in the open air.

At night John stabled the horses at a local inn. Foley, on perpetual guard with the dog, occupied the 'after-cabin'. The doctor was 'early to bed, early to rise', taking his beloved cold tub each morning with two buckets of cold water, an enormous sponge, a hunk of hard yellow soap, and a very hairy, rough towel the size of a double-bed sheet. He liked to set it up in the nearest patch of woodland, striding forth to his tub while the birds rushed madly away, with rooks cawing and wood-pigeons in a clatter of wings, amazed at this intrusion on their privacy.

Practical experience was vital to Stables's articles and tales. Without it, he was wordless. Everything he wrote has its own strong, bold, breezy tone. Victorian homes must have been frowsty places, with their elaborate drapes, thick carpets, heavy blankets and comforters, smoky open fires; there was undoubtedly a need for the fresh air Stables advocated so passionately. But it would be interesting to know his wife's reactions.

Time and again *B.O.P.*'s answers to correspondents rang with Dr Stables's praises of the Cold Tub, and his urgent plea to individual readers—'Take a cold tub, man!' The form of address was a magical touch. No youngster of spirit would resist the challenge, if by accepting it he could achieve manhood.

Below: an endpiece by Walter Mitton to a report on public-school athletics, by Charles J. B. Marriott, published on October 13, 1906 (Volume XXIX). Seventy-five years ago, when this first appeared in B.O.P., my father and one of his cousins were training hard for Rugby football. Three times a week in winter they jogged eight miles downhill from Halifax to Bradford. There they boarded a tram and rode home again, practising deep breathing on the upper deck, and on arrival rushed down to the cellar where two tin baths of cold water, drawn before they left, awaited them. Much splashing and larking about, a scrub with hard yellow soap, a rub-down with a hairy towel to restore the circulation: this was winter training in all weathers. In summer they made instead for the nearest natural 'swimming-hole', and after a healthy training run in the local park, plunged sternly into the water. This Cold Tub routine was taken in deadly seriousness, according to the pattern laid down in B.O.P. by Dr Stables and the best sporting experts of the day

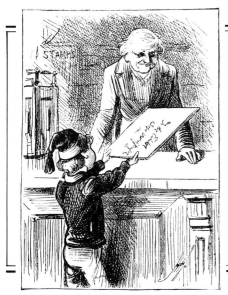

"How many stamps will that require, please Sir?"

Chapter Six
In the Highest Interests of our Correspondent

When Gordon composed the *Hutchison Memorial* in 1913, he singled out the regular *Answers to Correspondents* column, saying that it had kept *B.O.P.* in touch with boys all over the world:

Its publishers having facilities for distribution that competing journals could not hope for, it went to every corner of these islands, to every part of the empire, and beyond it. When the questions were on matters of interest to other readers they were answered through the paper, but when they were on strictly private matters—and the number of boys who looked on the editor as a confidential friend to whom they could open their hearts in all their doubts and difficulties was really surprising—they were replied to by letter; and often, perhaps years afterwards, words of cheer and notes of gratitude would come in, even from Polynesian islands, from those who had been enabled to resist temptation and kept in the right path by the Editor's timely advice.

This tribute to *B.O.P.*'s guidance was owed in no small measure to the persistence of the readers themselves, since the Editor stated over and over again that no replies would be sent by post. In the early days, readers were encouraged to send in their hobby queries, and they did so with enthusiasm. This not only provided a useful insight into likes and dislikes, but also helped to fill the pages with worthwhile copy free of charge, an important consideration. The correspondence column proved popular, and soon readers were writing in with requests for miscellaneous information.

Time and time again the Editor told readers that their requests and queries would only be answered in print, never by post, and that published replies could not possibly be given in 'the next number', since the magazine worked several weeks ahead. 'BERTIE CLERK will know by this time whether the squirrel is dead or alive' (March 17, 1888). The column consisted simply of a series of anonymous comments, each headed with the enquirer's initials or *nom de plume*. CONSTANT READER, SUBSCRIBER and WELL-WISHER were rebuked for choosing hackneyed names ('We never take any notice of letters so signed ... forty Constant Readers in a day! How *can* we assist you?'); FRIZZLY BACON, on the other hand, was repri-

Above: a line decoration from the correspondence columns, September 10, 1881 (*Volume III*)

manded for making so ugly a choice, and RED AND WHITE BLOTTING PAPER (1888) for using 'so ridiculous a tally'. Many readers chose the names of favourite heroes from serial stories.

Some of the 'answers' were extremely funny—and all the funnier because the original query was left to the imagination. In its first decade the magazine received on average three or four hundred letters a week. Some of these Mrs Hutchison answered in her husband's name. Some she passed to Gordon, Reed, Stables, Wood and other staff members or contributors, who scribbled their answers at the foot and returned them to her. Some replies were brusque to the point of rudeness. In 1880 REGULAR READER was slapped down: 'A man must *always* take the nationality of his father. Does your relative think he is a Welshman by any chance? If so he had better think again.' Other answers display a touch of spleen—'We are not sure of the colour of the South-Eastern Railway Carriages. The paint is rarely visible owing to the thick covering of dirt by which it is concealed' (July 28, 1888). But the majority were straightforward and informative. As time passed, increasingly curt reminders appeared, telling readers that their particular queries had already been answered in earlier issues—why, why, *why* didn't they check first?

From October 1879 to October 1880, the first complete twelve-month run of issues, *B.O.P.*'s readers asked for advice on preserving flowers; keeping rats, mice, chickens, pigeons, tortoises and canaries; bicycling and cricket. They requested and got, recipes for making sponge cakes, ginger beer, toffee, lemonade, strawberry ice cream and a surprisingly rich tipsy trifle ('Pour round it some white wines—raisin is very suitable—

Below: answers to readers' letters published on April 4, 1903 (Volume XXV)

Correspondence

"We want to know how, why, when. where, if," etc. etc.

E. P. H.—Wait until your voice is all right again, and by that time you may change your mind.

A READER OF THE "B.O.P." IN CANADA.—Thank you for your letter. It seemed rather odd that Frenchmen should wear kilts in Canada, but as the author stated that he had seen it we let the matter pass.

SPARK COIL.—If only to light the lamp for a short time at each operation, we think a dry battery would fulfil the conditions you name best. How to make one was given in No. 973 (September 4, 1897). You could buy one for about 3s. 6d. per cell.

S. S. A.—The information can be obtained from the Secretary to the Admiralty or the Secretary of the Civil Service Commission.

P. S. D.—The sole way to obtain now our coloured plate of Humming-Birds is to purchase the monthly part containing it (February part). If, as you say, you want it only for the time when you will bind your weekly numbers, you will be able to obtain it

ERNEST J. W.—We know of no stand camera as cheap as you require one. We think you should muster up your pecuniary forces until you can give at least 12s. 6d., at which price Hobbies, Limited, have one that will do good work. We would rather give 1l. and get a better class of hand camera—or a stand camera like Lancaster's "Le Merveilleux" is best of all for a beginner like yourself.

A. J. H. (Johannesburg)—As you get into better form the hair will probably strengthen without needing special attention. It is quite usual for the hair to fall out after a severe illness.

G. B. P. (Greenock).—1. Yes : it is always best to have the drawings made separate from the MS. 2. May be drawn large or small, as best suits the artist. Personally we prefer to receive them small size and to scale. 3. Payment usually depends on the value of the material submitted, the eminence of the author and value of his name, etc. ; but most journals of repute have a minimum scale.

CELT.—"Home Cricket" costs 8s. 6d., and can be had of Messrs. F. H. Ayres, the well-known game producers, 111 Aldersgate Street, London, E.C.

D. W. (Glasgow).—1. Read Mr. Bradshaw's recent articles in our pages on black-and-white drawing as a profession. They will supply just the sort of information you ask for. 2. You might begin by trying in our various drawing competitions. Some very well known artists of to-day began in this way, and we follow their successful career with great interest.

H. BUDGER.—Our first coloured plate was one of British butterflies, and in our eighteenth volume we had another coloured plate of every British species, reproduced from photographs of the same collection as that figured in "Our Country's Butterflies and Moths."

W. S.—You would probably hear of a book on acetylene gas by writing to Messrs. Spon, 125 Strand, W.C.

W. A. ADAMS.—The lantern glasses can be had from Dollond, Ludgate Hill (corner of Pilgrim Street), or Spiers & Pond (optical department), Queen Victoria Street (opposite St. Paul's station).

A. C. S.—1. The chances against it are too many to be called reasonable. 2. Stay where you are. 3. No difference in social position. 4. (a) The candidates are so numerous that the successes are about one in a hundred. (b) Ten or a dozen for each vacancy.

A. DEW.—We have had an article on coracle building. Some two feet deep.

J. SANSTER, G. IRESON, and others.—"How to Make a Fret-Saw" was in our seventeenth volume.

and a wineglassful of brandy'). They were dissuaded from making fire-works, coloured lights, lucifer matches and gunpowder. They were advised on coping with bunions, freckles, warts, chapped hands, pimples, blushing and stammering. (In later years the number of 'health' queries increased. The Editor tried to be cagey—in July, 1888, HOTSPUR was told 'You cannot safely treat rupture yourself', while the advice to W.H. WORTH in the same issue was brief and urgent, 'Consult a surgeon, and do so *soon*'—but Dr Stables was always willing to nail his colours to the mast, and gave advice on health with enthusiasm; it soon became his forte.) They asked for features on photography, geology, football, car-pentry, bookbinding, and pets. 'All in good time,' they were told; but readers who wanted lessons in Hebrew ('however brief'), French, Ger-man, Latin and shorthand were put firmly in their places: 'It would be making what is intended as a magazine of recreation too much like a school-book.' They sent specimens for identification—coins, stamps, birds' eggs and beetles. 'Your insect was smashed in the post,' the Editor told WILLIAM KINGSMILL, 'but we have identified the fragments as those of *Cetonia aurata*, the common rose-beetle. Next time you send us a speci-men, put it in a box.'

Readers were convinced that there must be *some* practical or profitable end to which they could put used stamps, and the Editor became very tetchy as he told them, time and again, that there was not. He was also plagued by enquiries for back numbers and presentation plates, and requests from readers wanting to get their copies bound. Instead of questions about hobbies, leisure interests and information of general interest, he got manuscripts of poems and stories, and endless appeals for his opinion of correspondents' handwriting and his advice on careers they might pursue.

D.A.C.—Your writing is quite good enough for a merchant's office, but a little more care in the crossing of your t's and the formation of your o's would improve it.

J.C.—Even if your writing were good enough, your spelling most certainly is not.

H.R. (Coventry)—Your writing would be considered fairly good for commercial purposes; it is not firm and bold enough for the law.

S.W.A.—The fact of your being a tradesman's son would not, of itself, be a bar to your becoming an officer in the army; but a far higher standard of education would be required than, to judge from your letter, you possess. 'Rigment,' 'standered,' 'standerd' and 'tradman' are dreadful! . . . The Engineers, as you are fond of 'making *skeetches*', might suit you.

Readers of the early *B.O.P.* longed to be soldiers of the Queen. They wrote in for advice on the height and chest measurements, the educational standard required, the special qualifications needed by a military bands-man or a trumpeter. An intriguing reply went to J.B.S.T.—'We are afraid that, under the circumstances, you have no chance of entering the army as an officer. You certainly would not be allowed to keep your parentage and place of birth secret' (1888). The Navy, too, had a host of willing recruits. Other boys wanted to be clerks (it was the Editor's opinion that this was an over-crowded occupation). Some of the most interesting

G. VAN CASTELL.—The articles on Thought-Reading were in the third volume, which has been out of print for years, and can only be had second-hand, probably through an advertisement in our wrapper or in "Exchange and Mart."

E. A. SCOTT.—We have had no article on lantern-slides since that which appeared in May 1898, but the subject will be taken up again.

A FOLKESTONIAN MONTHLY SUBSCRIBER.—1. The machine so made would be of such little use that you would simply be wasting the rubber letters. 2. See the article on the new signal code in the number for October 5, 1901.

J. W. SHARPE, R. A. WALTER, and L. E. A.—Attend the Board of Education Science Classes in Geometrical Drawing and Machine Construction and Drawing.

GOLLYWOGS.—A gollywog is a common sort of doll.

H. ELDRIDGE and STEVE.—Nothing satisfactory. In removing the blot with weak oxalic acid and bleaching the paper with chloride of lime, the remedy would seem to be worse than the disease.

P. F. N.—The volume is out of print with us, but you might get a copy by advertising.

S. K. (St. Bees) writes to point out an unfortunate transposition in a recent article on "School Football Doings." "It is therein made to appear that Carlisle beat St. Bees by 44 pts. to 8 ; it was St. Bees that beat Carlisle by that margin."

MISSING LINK (Crosby).—1. Some competitions are held monthly—the " Descriptive," for example—and others are announced from time to time. Full details are usually given in every November part. 2. It is called the December part obviously because it is issued for that particular month.

INTERESTED.—The 18th volume, whether in numbers or parts, is quite out of print with us, but copies might perhaps be obtained by advertising on the wrappers of either our weekly or monthly issues—at a cost of 3d. and 6d. respectively.

E. C. GRIGSON (Adelaide).—1. It is not a matter of great importance. They should be slightly thicker than those given for the small dynamo—say No. 16 for magnet and 14 for armature. 2. Probably from 15 to 20 volts. 3. Size of wire for core, No. 22 ; core ¾ in. diameter and 5½ in. long. Wire for primary, 18 B.W.G., four layers. Wire for secondary, No. 38, amount about 1 lb. With a condenser it might give 1 in. spark ; it will want four or five bichromate batteries.

J. WATSON.—You cannot get a really good camera for

replies, in social history terms, were to apprentices. The first three given here are from Volume II, 1879–80; the fourth from 1888.

G.G.T. (York)—Depend upon it, for an apprentice to talk too much of 'rights' and what he can 'claim' in the way of holidays is a serious mistake. It is much better from every point of view to try what conciliation will do.

JAMES TIMEWELL.—Your letter about hours of work is written in a very proper spirit, and we can but think that a little respectful remonstrance with your master, while at the same time showing a willing obedience, would sooner or later have the desired effect.

AN ANXIOUS MOTHER wishes to know 'if an ironmonger can compel his apprentices to be behind the counter till nine o'clock one evening and ten another night.' In the absence of specified hours in the indentures, we should say that a master, whether ironmonger or not, would expect his apprentices' services during the usual hours of business. The hours mentioned certainly seem late, but there may be indulgence on the other side of which we know nothing. Speaking broadly, we should say that nothing will be gained by the apprentice standing too much upon his 'rights.' 'Better for a man that he wear the yoke in his youth.'

E.C. BARK.—Fifteen hours a day is, we consider, much too long for a boy of fourteen to have to work; but we do not see what you can do except complete your apprenticeship. You should not have chosen a trade in which such long hours are necessary.

Many readers of the Victorian *B.O.P.* were in urgent need of adult advice. Diffident about speaking freely to parents and older relatives,

Above: Walter Mitton's heading for the correspondence column, June 27, 1904 (Volume XXV)

hesitant about approaching schoolmasters, clergymen and doctors, they turned to the *B.O.P.* with touching confidence. Reading between the lines of *Answers to Correspondents*, it seems as if their sad, ingenuous, hopeful letters spoke of personal problems at school or home, worries about health, difficulties faced in their everyday working lives, and, in veiled terms, the sexual frustration inevitable given the social and moral structures of the time. ('BAD HABITS, Anxious.—Very sorry. But boys who do so kill all manhood, and the intellect is never what it should be'— on such lines ran hundreds of replies, this particular one appearing in April, 1905.) Some of the correspondents were evidently in their early twenties, with schooldays well behind them. In 1905, among the 'hobby' replies, is one to F.M. (Brentwood), who must surely have been over twenty-one: 'If you wish to buy a house there are many genuine building societies from which you could choose. Two of the best are the National Freehold Land and Building Society of Moorgate Street, City, and the Temperance Permanent Building Society in Ludgate Hill, E.C.' *B.O.P.* was always ready and willing to encourage thrift.

The replies printed in the magazine were at their most serious and sincere on the rare occasions when they were dealing with religious conviction. Most of the other replies have a bracing tone, which can become uncomfortably jaunty. CAVALRYMAN was urged not to dream of becoming a field-marshal but to limit his 'notions severely to that of sergeant' (January 14, 1888). LANCASHIRE LAD and SANDY MAC, who hoped for assisted passages to the colonies 'for a year or two', to look things over, were sternly told to stay at home: 'You are not the sort of immigrant that the colonials would appreciate, and your availing yourself of their help simply to inspect them would be, in plain English, a fraud.' HERBERT, an aspiring writer, had to take it on the chin: 'It is extremely unlikely that Victor Hugo would ever answer any of your letters, even if we forwarded them. He has been dead quite some years.' But other 'miscellaneous' replies were distinguished by an admirable thoroughness which sounds very like Gordon. One of my favourites appeared in Volume XL, 1917–18, and is surely attributable to him: 'The character you mention was so popular among readers that the same publisher issued *Ching Ching's Own*★. To give it a start a competition was devised, the prize being a semi-detached house. This house, in Leathwaite Road, Battersea Rise, was called Ching Ching's Villa, and bore the name for some years.' Who could resist such meticulous service? In 1903 E.E. STARKEY was told, 'We are very sorry, but we find it quite impossible to discover the fault in your son's accumulator, and as the instructions were given in another paper, now non-existent, we do not see what assistance is possible. Accumulators often require to be charged slightly and discharged again several times before they will take the full charge properly. The fact of the acid bubbling proves that some action took place. As it happens, you are only a few miles from Mr S. R. Bottone, of Wallington, so we recommend you to consult him. He is always kind in giving assistance to the aspiring amateur.'

Stables's advice was always powerful stuff and its tone is unmistakable.

★ *Ching Ching's Own* was published by Charles Fox's *Boy's Standard* in 1888; its wily oriental hero was created by E. Harcourt Burrage.

'Paint all the warts at once with *very strong* nitric acid. Ensure none gets on the skin.' As an ex-Naval doctor, he was particularly exasperated by the unceasing flood of enquiries about careers at sea. 'R. FINDLAY WILSON' and many others were told, 'Oh, yes; oh, yes; and it is all in [the booklet] *The Sea*. What is the use of a reader who does not read?' (January, 1905). When one reader caught him out misquoting Shakespeare, the reply pointed a moral: 'We commend you on your feat. We quote freely from Shakespeare and other bardies from time to time and sometimes memory plays us false. We then own up *like men*.' A boy with a mysterious complaint, 'darkness in the eyes', was told that he might easily have 'darkness in the heart' as well—'That's a plain fact,' said Stables cheeringly.

Health queries became his major field of interest. 'PERSPIRING TOO FREELY (C.J.R.).—Boys of your age often do. It shows they are under par. Plenty of exercise and fresh air. No physic' (October, 1904). 'DREAMS (G.K.)—Natural, unless you have given way to bad habits. These and smoking are doing untold mischief' and on the same page 'T.M. MACY wishes to have white hands. What does a boy want with such girlish things? Yes. Oatmeal-water, and lemon-juice rubbed in at night. The cold morning tub to strengthen the circulation *and* outdoor exercise' (December, 1904). 'SWIMMING IN WINTER (Mac.).—Few can stand it, but judge for yourself if you can get a good reaction. Dr Gordon Stables tells us that he joined his swimming club in December when a student. Keeps it up all the year round. Has swum for his life with his heavy clothes on in the Arctic regions. Took no hurt. Others might' (January, 1905). SPARTAN wrote boldly, saying that *warm* baths were the order of the day in his home and he had never suffered any ill-effects; he was curtly rebuked: 'Have you *no* inventive faculties?' HIRSUTE, who longed for a fine pair of whiskers, was told that 'a really cold tub' was the only hope. H.G., Cambridgeshire, was dismissed with brutal candour—he was 'much too old to get rid of bow legs'—while FOOLISH was sharply dealt with— 'Once tattooed, always tattooed. No wonder you sign yourself "Foolish".' Fresh air, cold tubs, oatmeal, virol and phospherine: these were the cures for readers' ills. 'NERVES (J.A.M.)—You had better try virol and phospherine to set you up. Cleanliness of mind and body, fresh air and cold bath' (October 1904).

In the summer of 1905, Stables himself fell ill ('The Doctor has been down with influenza and inflammation for long weeks') but he reappeared with his opinions unmodified: 'Rise not later than 7 and cold tub immediately. In very cold weather massage yourself all over before turning out, and then with the rough towel after the cold tub. Breakfast at 8, but only after ten minutes in the open air.' One cannot help feeling that the renowned doctor came off second-best in the case of TARANAKI, the colourful *nom de plume* of a New Zealand reader who asked for something to help his nerves. He was told sternly, as one might have expected, to 'take plenty of exercise in the open air and a cold tub every morning before breakfast,' but was not very enthusiastic, and reappeared in the correspondence column some months later. 'It is very difficult to get a cold tub in New Zealand, sir. Our country is full of hot springs, natural springs. What shall I do?' (for once the letter was quoted as well

Above: Between Ourselves, *a feature written by Sid G. Hedges, was introduced in January, 1940, the Padre's Talk (facing page) having been brought to an end in December, 1939. Hedges invited his readers to write to him about anything that might be weighing on their minds. General topics would be discussed in the column; personal queries would receive a private reply—* 'Problems of which things are right and not right, of conscience, continence, honesty, ambition, belief, sociability, sex, language, religion, leisure.' *The first topics to occupy the column were friendship; frankness about pregnancy and the facts of life; choosing a career; and whether to say grace before meals*

The post-War years still brought 'perplexed and sometimes distressing letters' from troubled readers. In March, 1953, during my own editorship, McEwan Lawson contributed an article on the sex instinct. Sex hunger, he pointed out, was as natural as hunger for food. He told readers to try thinking about other people's needs rather than their own immediate pleasure; to put their faith in spiritual values; not to use girls for their own gratification or to think of them only in terms of sex; and, on a practical note which the trenchant Stables would surely have endorsed, he added, 'When sexual desire comes flooding in don't go on dozing or dreaming. Get up and do something active'

as the reply). Stables played for time: 'We will think about it and let you have a private reply by post, although this is *not* our normal practice *and we cannot do so again.*' No more was ever heard about Taranaki and his nerves.

Another reader, SCRIPTUS, had evidently pointed out the difficulties of following the doctor's routine if there was no tub in the house. Stables took that one in his stride: 'Douche yourself regularly 365 days a year in the mornings on rising, and 366 in any Leap Year, with 30 sponge loads of the coldest water obtainable. We presume there is somewhere around where you can do this with discretion.' Determined that the reader should be under no false illusions, Stables added as a footnote: 'The water must be *really cold.*' Meanwhile BEAVER of Northern Ontario was urged: '*On no account* should you ever cut a circular hole in the winter ice to get a cold tub. You would certainly freeze to death very quickly but it is also probable you might well provide a tasty meal for some hungry seal lurking below. In your case, wait for the spring thaws.'

Some two years after *B.O.P.* was launched, Stables began to contribute a famous regular feature, *Doings for the Month*, which first appeared in November 1881. Despite its cramped type and the lack of decorative artwork, *Doings* became one of the most successful items in the magazine. It was a series of practical short pieces under sub-headings: The Garden and Window Box, Poultry Run, Pigeon Loft, Aviary, Rabbitry, Apiary and Kennel. The Editor probably hoped that it would divert the flood of enquiries about sickly pets which came in week by week. Stables did not hesitate to use the Cold Tub technique on pets, too, if necessary. S.V.F. had a parrot which was losing its feathers (April, 1905). 'No wonder!' thundered the doctor on learning what food S.V.F. gave his pet. '*Scalded Indian corn, indeed!* Guess you would lose *your* feathers on such a diet. Get a proper parrot mixture and give clean water daily for bath and drinking.' Bantams needed green grass, sunshine and, inevitably, oatmeal ('draggled with milk'). Poor CECIL incurred the doctor's wrath in full measure: 'You obviously know absolutely nothing about canaries. Find a good home for them all at once.' Stables always knew exactly where he stood, and he took an admirable stand against docking puppies' tails ('cruel and no prevention of distemper'), wheels in rats' cages ('arrant cruelty') and caged songbirds—'We decline to give any instructions for such cruelty as imprisoning skylarks in cages. Be content with the mischief you have done, and do it no more.'

From 1896 onwards, *Doings for the Month* was expanded to include notes on the health and happiness of 'the Boy Himself'. Correspondents were frequently urged to consult these instead of wasting space in the Answers to Correspondents column. 'EVIL HABITS (To Several).—Read back "Doings" etc. We cannot answer every week on these. If you strictly follow Dr Gordon Stables' monthly health talks in "Doings" you will be the gainers' (November, 1904). A typical *Doings* broadside of March, 1905, began in formidable terms:

Look here, lads! Eyes front! Stand at ease! Now *listen.* It has been stated publicly, after careful observation and investigation, that the girls of the rising generation are far better set up, far stronger and healthier, and of course, therefore, happier, than the boys of England and the boys of Scotland who live

MAY.

THE PIGEON LOFT.— We told you last month that the newly-hatched birds would not be much to look at. But it is wonderful how soon they grow when the parents get wheat, and the best of peas and tares, and small tick beans, with a morsel of green food, and plenty of clean gravel and water.

Footers we mentioned. They are, when young, apt to get weak in the legs. It is not an accident. It is from weakness, and I doubt if it be curable. It is only another proof that we cannot feed the parents too well, and in addition we should let plenty of sunlight into our lofts. The young of pigeons get like porcupines in six or seven days if all be well, and these quills open into feathers after about ten days. In a month's time the young ought to be as big as the old.

THE RABBITRY.— Is all right here? If not, depend upon it it is the owner's fault. We were at a house some evenings ago where the boys had recently purchased at a sale the back numbers, bound, of the B. O. P. One of them told us the Editor was always down on rabbit-keepers. He did not know, and does not know, he was talking to this cruel Editor. We had a look at his rabbitry next day, and were pleased to find it A1, and the bunnies all happy and full-eyed, glossy and sleek, no bad smell, and no dirty troughs. Why should it not be always like this? Boys go away sometimes—this applies to all fancies—and leave their pets to the care of servants. This is wrong. It is best for two boys, or a boy and his sister, to go halves in a fancy, and one "pard" should always be at home.

THE KENNEL.— Read last month's DOINGS.

THE BEE WORLD.— Swarming may be expected this month or early next. It depends on the weather and latitude. June is the month far north. You will want a lesson or two more than ever now about this important branch. Get it from some bee-keeper, for even book knowledge has its drawbacks. If the weather be cold and inclement feed still.

THE KITCHEN GARDEN.— Sow peas again for rotation. Weed and thin your beds and drills. Sow greens still in spare corners. Plant celery in deep, well manured trenches, and tomatoes from your hot bed. Put them against hot, sheltered walls. If you have a whitewashed wall all the better. Sow French beans, and put in vegetable-marrow plants. Keep all clean and tidy.

THE FLOWER AND WINDOW GARDENS.— Get your beds ready, and plant out your annuals about the second week in this month. Zinnias and dwarf asters, and Tom Thumb nasturtiums, make a pretty show. They must have manure, though, and sun and water. Plant geraniums later on. Attend to

in cities. The physical degeneration of the inhabitants of this kingdom, then, is nearly all on the male side. Our sailors (Royal Navy) are good men and true. The hardiness of their upbringing would account for this. They are caught young, and there is no better physical nor mental education in the world than that which they receive on training ships and on short cruises. Moreover, they are well fed and kept clean and wholesome. Nor is it only our East-End boys who are deteriorating, but West-Enders also. It is want of suitable food, cleanliness and home comforts generally that keeps down the poor slum children, added to vice easily acquired from the example of their elders and from reading the penny dreadfuls issued by the guttersnipe press. Then come school vices, and these are as common in West-End schools as in the gloomy East-End. Of course such vices emasculate the young, and boys become weazen-faced old men by the time they reach the age of thirty. Smoking adds to the miserable conditions of growing lads, but I ought hardly to say growing, for grow they do not, neither to height nor breadth of beam. The children of the wealthy and well-to-do in cities are apt to be spoiled by pampering and coddling and over-feeding. Cargoes of such little fat boys would sell well in some parts of New Guinea, but in this country they do not assist in the very least to keep the crown on the King's head. Now, lads ... give up smoking at once and bad habits of all sorts. They will kill you as surely as a falling brick kills a beetle!

In spite of the existence of *B.O.P.*'s sister publication, the *Girl's Own Paper*, to which Stables contributed regular articles on health and beauty under the pseudonym 'Medicus', many girls read *B.O.P.*, tried their luck

Above: here is Dr Stables's advice for the month of May, 1888 (Volume X). This also included 'thirteen truths' about keeping canaries ('Do not bother with artificial eggs, canaries are not fools')

CORRESPONDENCE

M. SMALLEY.—A George III. sovereign of 1820, if in good condition, is worth five-and-twenty shillings.

WILF.—You might get the information you want from the Emigrants' Information Office, 31 Broadway, Westminster.

ANXIOUS.—You cannot be a boy clerk for ever. The appointment is one that only lasts a few years. The usual course is to study during the time so as to be able to pass for the Second Division.

BOY CLERK.—The Examination Papers for all Government situations are obtained from Rees, Limited, booksellers, Pall Mall, opposite the Carlton Hotel.

HEREFER.—The Great Eastern Railway Company issue such maps and guides at a nominal charge. Apply to the Manager, Continental Department, Liverpool Street, E.C.

ARABIC.—There is no book, but we have had a large number of articles on Kites and Kite flying.

M. GURNEY.—Thomas Atkins is the specimen name used in the form a soldier has to sign on enlistment. For the Thomas Atkins his own name is substituted.

W. H. COX.—No licence is required, but it is not a reputable occupation, and those engaged in it are more or less under the surveillance of the police.

HERBERT G. COOK, H. BALLEY, and others.—We regret that we are really quite unable to help you in the choice of an occupation. Other readers please note.

J. L. ROSE, H. WOOD, and others.—Buy "The Sea," fifteen-pence, post free, published at "The Shipping Gazette" Office, 54 Gracechurch Street, E.C.

S. W. JEFFREY.—1. You will find all about them, with coloured illustrations, in "Our Country's Birds" and its supplement, "Eggs of the Native birds of Britain," which any bookseller can supply you with. 2. Quite so—or thereabouts.

P. HARVEY.—The first series of articles was in our fourth volume, and there have been several since; in fact, there has been something about the matter in nearly every volume.

F. C. F.—Look down the list of books published by Vinton & Co. at the "Agricultural Gazette" Office, Bream's Buildings, Chancery Lane.

AN AGED SUBSCRIBER.—It is a subject for an article and not for an answer, and we have made a note of it.

DEVOTEE.—There are several books on lawn-tennis. Perhaps that by H. A. Vaile would give you the hints you require, and you can get it from any bookseller.

A. READ.—Too large a subject to be entered upon here. We will return to it shortly from a new point of view.

A. M. ADAMS.—We had a series of articles in an early volume, giving the dimensions of all the gores, etc., and reprinted them in our " Indoor Games."

STUTTERING (L. A.).—Nervousness. Needs treatment for a long time by an expert. Strengthen the constitution by regular living, good food, the cold bath, and a course of phosferine. Take time to talk.

TEETH AND THE SERVICES (C. C. R.).—Yes, if so many as you mention were decayed you would hardly pass for the Navy or Army. But see an Army surgeon or a Navy one.

RED NOSE (W. D.).—It may be from indigestion, so mind what you eat and drink. But more often it is a weakness or laxity in the capillary blood-vessels of the organ, and then no doctor can cure it.

SHORT-WINDED (G. P.).—You want to have your chest examined by a doctor. Cannot advise any self-treatment in such a case.

G. MILBURN.—There are several such in " The Boy's Own Reciter."

BLACKHEADS (W. G.).—Wash the face or sponge it with hot water, then, having well dried your hands, squeeze the disfigurements out and rub in a little zinc ointment at night. Cold-water douche to the face thrice daily.

W. S. (Melb., Australia).—The drawings are scarcely up to our standard for publication. Thanks.

LANKY.—See answer to J. B. You must be at a funny sort of school if they prohibit the bath. We can hardly credit it.

SECRET VICE (A. J. J.).—You are in a bad way, and should consult your own family doctor.

TORTOISES (O. Z. C.)—Read back, please.

R. E. ROBINS.—The river Loddon rises near Basingstoke, in some ponds called Nervram Springs, but the fishing is private. We remember catching a number of roach in the canal, years ago; but even this has ceased to be free, we fancy. Still, you should be able to obtain, by local inquiry, details as to ownership, etc., and possibly might get a day's leave.

G. and S. K. (Budapest).—We were delighted to receive your letter, as we are always glad to hear from distant readers. The writer made his journey from Bucharest to Budapest.

CARLO (Scarboro').—All the matters you name will be treated in our next volume, which begins the first week in October.

CONSTANT READER.—Certainly not. To use in that way copyright stories that may take your fancy would get you into very serious trouble.

NEW CHUM (Canterbury).—The "B.O.P." volume closes with the September numbers (October part), and the new volume begins with the first week in October. The "E.B.M." volume, on the other hand, runs from January to December of each year.

RABBITS (Hilda S.).—Best oats, crusts of bread, succulent roots like carrot, parsnip, turnip, etc., green food, hay in its rack, and now and then a bran-mash. If you write to Spratt's Patent, Fenchurch Street, and mention this paper, they will send you a small, handy book on rabbits.

GOLD FISH (R. H.).—Your fish is moribund, owing to your unskilful treatment. No boy should take charge of a pet until he has found out its proper treatment. It is very cruel and sinful. "Only a fish," you may say, but even fish have their feelings.

RIDGE (High Barnet).—1. Better wait until you are 18, or even 21. 2. We are not in want of writers.

C. E. H.—Yes, a course of phosferine for your nervousness, and the cold tub, early hours, and plenty of outdoor exercise.

BELOW MEASUREMENT FOR NAVY (J. B.).—1. Learn to swim, and swim daily: good food, and Virol after every meal. 2. A mixed diet, but never over-eat. That makes a boy sluggish and foolish. "Fit" doesn't necessarily mean strength. In measuring the chest, naval officers do so over the skin, and do not tighten it very hard!

in the competitions (despite attempts to dissuade them) and wrote hopefully to the Editor. Stables's answers to girl readers were characteristic. 'Yes, 5 feet 10¾ inches *is* a good height for a girl of 14. Cheer up, Agnes!—you can't cheer down!' (January 14, 1905). A girl who had the effrontery to call herself TOMMIE 'wanted to get strong like the boys. Can you please suggest a scheme?' Stables replied with his archest tone and favourite remedy: 'Have you tried the really cold tub and the *B.O.P.* dumb-bell exercises every morning before breakfast, my dear?' Sadly there was no further reference to Tommie. Did the combination of cold tubs and dumb-bells prove too much for her on typically British mornings? Or did she survive and prosper, thanks to *B.O.P.*?

Some of the appeals for help must surely have been spoofs. I can readily believe that lively undergraduates or slick young City gents, who had revelled in *B.O.P.* as schoolboys, thought it fun to bait the dour Scottish doctor with his well-known eccentricities. In general, though, Stables' integrity overcame criticism and parents approved of his sterling advice. Cold tubs, open windows, vigorous exercise, hard walking and manly pursuits all went down well. But occasionally Stables over-reached himself. A mild-mannered Canadian received the icy retort, 'You are far too old for the Navy and you had better remain where you are ... out in Manitoba where you could grow wheat or something' (very much the Stables tone). AMBITIOUS was told, 'Judging from your letter we should say it would be a sheer waste of time applying for *any* post.' The most celebrated case occurred on October 25, 1902, in a summary reply to an unhappy reader: 'BAD HABITS (F.D.)—Coffins are cheap and boys like you are not of much use in the world. We do not answer by post.' On this occasion Hutchison was admonished by the Society for lack of editorial control in allowing 'an answer which would have been improper in *any* paper'. Called before the Committee, he apologised on his own and the writer's behalf. A modified reply appeared in the *Boy's Own Annual* for that year—'If you go on as you are, there is nothing before you but an early and dishonoured grave. Pray God to forgive and help you to resist temptation.' The Committee minutes recorded that 'a grave error of judgment had been committed ... but it was in the highest interests of their correspondent.'

The magazine's treatment of its correspondents in the Victorian and Edwardian years was in direct contrast to the modern style. In my own days as Editor, by which time *B.O.P.* had become a monthly periodical, I read all the readers' letters myself. Selected letters were quoted in the magazine (condensed if necessary), each with a brief reply from myself or one of our hobby or sporting experts. We frequently published readers' letters on advertisement pages, since advertising revenue was our life-blood. From time to time we ran 'For' and 'Against' letters on issues of the day. We also offered our readers an inducement: every letter published earned a minimum of seven shillings and sixpence (37½p) for the sender, while the 'star' items earned anything from ten shillings (50p) to two pounds. Hutchison would have been astonished.

Above: a column of readers' letters published in the issue of March, 1951, during my own time as Editor

Far left: in contrast, a page of correspondence from the Hutchison era, published on August 31, 1907 (Volume XXIX)

Chapter Seven

Mr G.A.Hutchison, Editor

Above: a line decoration from the issue of September 24, 1881 (Volume III)

Far right: the opening of a short story from the latter years of the Hutchison era; A Climb to Remember, by Charles Edwardes, was published on October 9, 1909 (Volume XXXII). Neddy's bullying uncle calls him 'Miss Girl Face', a 'misfit in trousers', a milksop and a coward; and when, after supper, the boy reads aloud a sea story in which one of the characters has a fight with a shark—the sort of incident featured not infrequently in B.O.P.—Uncle boils over. 'What'd you have done? Slipped down the varmint's throat without a kick, I'll be bound.' Poor Neddy dashes out into the night and is groping through the dark when something strikes his right shoulder. Flinging up his hands, he catches hold of a rope and is whisked from the ground. He has been carried off by two balloonists making an experimental flight (at dead of night!) and his painful struggle to swarm up the rope to the basket is indeed a climb to remember

The death of Reed was a severe blow to Hutchison, and shortly afterwards Ballantyne, another valued writer, also died. Fortunately the magazine was, by this time, well established in the eyes of the public.

During the first decade of the paper's life, sales remained good. The figures of the time were not audited and certified as correct by any independent body, but I would accept them as broadly accurate. In its first year, according to the minutes, B.O.P. made a profit of £2,499 16s. 8d., second only to the established *Sunday at Home*. The second year was even better, making a profit of £2,626. Unhappily, neither the Committee minutes, nor the minutes of the Finance Sub-Committee, are consistent in recording sales and circulation figures, but there are occasional references and one of these (June 26, 1884) gives the circulation at that time as 57,000 weekly issues and 90,000 monthly parts. The difference between circulation and readership figures is always difficult to assess, but there can be no doubt that the latter figure was considerably higher. A quarter of a million is a fair estimate, and was the figure quoted in the fiftieth anniversary issue, of 1929.

Many boys bought their own copies every Saturday with their precious pennies. Others were given theirs by indulgent fathers who brought home half a dozen papers and periodicals from the city bookstall for family reading. Many headmasters thoroughly approved of B.O.P. and allowed pupils to subscribe to the paper. On the occasion of the fiftieth anniversary, older readers recalled that in some schools the boys were paraded and presented with a copy apiece of the first issue, to whet their appetites. Less fortunate city youngsters could read it in the local free library, and in parts of the country children were encouraged to attend Sunday School regularly by getting B.O.P. and G.O.P. as their 'reward'. My own father, born in 1890, spent his early schooldays in Lincolnshire and was given a copy every Sunday at his Wesleyan Methodist Sunday School. It was usually three or four weeks old but no one worried about that. His older sister received a copy of G.O.P. in the same way. When the family moved to Lancashire in 1900 the same system applied at their new Sunday School, but here competition was fiercer. The only way to be *sure* of getting your copy in Manchester was to order and pay for it! The Sunday Schools helped Christian magazines considerably by buying and distributing copies in days when competition was intense and promotion as we know it hardly existed—though the Society had been careful to issue a tempting prospectus when launching *B.O.P.*, and in October 1879, nine months later, cannily arranged that W. H. Smith's should display *B.O.P.*'s Contents List at 400 station bookstalls at a fee of £1 per station per year, for five years.

Despite the encouraging sales and circulation figures, and the fine style in which *B.O.P.* and *G.O.P.* progressed, the Society seemed not wholly satisfied. They praised the magazines' content and the skill and talent displayed in writing, editing and producing them, but warned the editorial staff to be on the watch 'lest the ventures become corrupted by their environment on the bookstalls'. Pointed references to the 'solemn responsibilities' of the Editor-in-Chief reminded James Macaulay in no uncertain terms of his supervisory duties. Poor Macaulay, now in his seventies, had so much work on his plate with *Leisure Hour* and *Sunday at Home* that he was thankful to trust *B.O.P.* and *G.O.P.* to the good sense and ability of Hutchison and Peters. In November, 1879, he expressed his wish to resign the editorship of *B.O.P.* into Hutchison's hands, but the Committee would not agree; and he was not in fact released from his formal responsibility for *B.O.P.* and *G.O.P.*, at a supervision fee of £100 per paper, for another eighteen years.

In a critical assessment of *B.O.P.* and *G.O.P.* recorded in the Committee minutes for April 8, 1884, the Committee expressed the opinion that the space given to fiction would be better devoted to 'travel and adventures in real life, papers in history, and in the biography of the wise and the good, which would be useful in forming character as well as affording pleasant reading'. In asking for 'more prominence to Christian truth and influence', the Society stressed the main purpose for which the magazines had been founded, and with such a dedicated team of editors this at least was hardly necessary. 'Let's do our best,' said Hutchison in characteristic reply, 'and get on with the job for there is much to do.'

In the eighteen-nineties the Society's magazines ran into trouble, as did their competitors. *Sunday at Home* and *Leisure Hour* were forced to close in 1894, after several years of sharp decline. *B.O.P.* began the decade in profit—in 1890 it made £4,707, an increase of nearly £700 over the previous year; but its sales, too, had begun to fall, and in the eight months from April to December, 1891, they dropped by 57,000. Its sister publication, *G.O.P.*, which had outstripped it in the early years, continued to sell the better of the two—probably because of the range of its readership. *G.O.P.*'s correspondence columns, its articles and features, and its serial stories (very few of which have schoolgirl heroines), all make it clear that *G.O.P.* was bought by young wives, working girls and domestic servants, as well as schoolgirls. But *G.O.P.*, too, suffered from the decline in revenue. *B.O.P.* remained in profit until 1897, when for the first time it made a gross profit (£5,242) but a net loss (£1,407); *G.O.P.*'s net profit was down to £993.

The same year saw Macaulay's retirement. After nearly twenty years'

It was a blustering night; so dark that even Neddy's sharp eyes could see nothing. Ere he was five steps down the lane he was into the hedge. The ditch first, which gave the hedge brambles a fine chance to scratch his face. He was almost in tears when he rushed out of his Uncle Emmanuel's cottage, with the valiant, but rather hollow, determination to run away because he couldn't bear any more of it.

The most he really meant to do was to get as far as Tommy Shafto's home at the other side of Camberbury's green. Tommy's mother and grandmother, and even Tommy's sisters three, had often expressed their sympathy that such a nice boy as Neddy should have to live with a relation like Emmanuel Boon, whose tongue nearly always had its rough side uppermost. Tommy's mother once said that Mr. Boon didn't deserve to be called captain—he was so harsh with his nephew. But as a retired sea skipper he was certainly entitled to the courtesy prefix, even though he had only one natural leg, a red face, and such rough notions about hammering boys into useful men.

The trouble to-night was about Neddy's want of common old-fashioned enterprise, and what his uncle termed "Spirit and spunk!" From the summerhouse on the field side of the garden, the captain had that evening seen Neddy come home from the sawmill, where he was just beginning to earn money. Farmer Dolland's bull was out at grass close to the path, and Neddy had made three cautious tacks across the meadow to spare the bull the excitement of seeing him. The bull didn't so much as lift his head, but the moment he was at home Neddy's uncle was upon him as afflictingly almost as a bull, with charges about his lack of courage.

"When I was your age, I'd the fear of nothing in me," snapped the uncle. "I'd have twisted that animal's tail sooner than sneak round him like a little cur. You, with two sound young legs, Edward, to do a thing like that! I don't know what your generation's coming to, if you're a fair sample."

It was never any good arguing with Uncle

"I'M SORRY, Grant, but you will not do."

"Won't do? What do you mean?"

"I mean that I shall have to put Ashmore in to row number one. As I say, I'm sorry, but I dare not trust you."

Jack Royal spoke as if he really were sorry, but this did not soften the blow to the other boy's pride.

Wellminster was to fight for the supremacy of the River Ouse with the rival school of Montford on the morrow, and Royal, who, besides being captain of the rowing-club, also pulled "stroke" in the racing-boat and acted as coach, was anxious about the work of each of his men.

"Why can't you trust me?" demanded Grant, gazing wistfully at the graceful four-oared cutter in which a trial spin had just been finished, and which was rocking gently against the landing-stage of the boat-house.

"It is simple enough," replied Royal. "We were six minutes covering that mile just now, and we should have done it in five-forty, at most, if the bow oar had been steady."

"I rowed as well as I could."

"Exactly. You rowed as well as you could, and that is why I must make a change at the eleventh hour. If there were hope of you doing better in the race it would be unnecessary. The honour of Wellminster School comes before everything. We must win this race."

Above: the opening of another short story from the Edwardian period; Almost a Traitor *by George C. Jenks appeared in three parts, August 10–24, 1907 (Volume XXIX). It was a rowing story, with sullen Grant replaced at bow by clean-limbed young Ashmore, and driven by sheer disappointment to try an unworthy revenge*

service Hutchison was at last confirmed in his true title, as Editor, and three years later he had the great satisfaction of enjoying the Coming-of-Age Dinner in London, organised by Gordon and Mr W. D. Lines at the Holborn Restaurant and felicitously arranged for Hutchison's birthday, October 31, 1899. All *B.O.P.*'s contributors and artists were invited to dine on soup, sole, whitebait, mutton cutlets and turkey, apricots, jelly and ice pudding. The Archdeacon of London took the chair and spoke of the paper's 'wonderful power for good in raising the moral tone of the youth of our nation both at home and abroad'. Hutchison was a powerful and eloquent speaker on any platform (Baptist lay preacher, Sunday School superintendent, Liberal politician) and he replied in sincere terms. 'For twenty-one years we here, all of us, have worked together with a definite purpose to help boys to live straight. Often and often boys in trouble write to me frankly about themselves. It has ever been my aim and joy to advise to the best of my ability, and to aid in the making of manly God-fearing citizens. I have received many proofs from all parts of the English-speaking world that the work has not been in vain.' An even greater concourse was to gather twenty-nine years later for the paper's Golden Jubilee Luncheon, when the Prime Minister of the day, Stanley Baldwin, proposed the toast 'Prosperity to the *Boy's Own Paper*' and was photographed reading the current issue of *B.O.P.* as he walked over Westminster Bridge. Hutchison had died some years before, but his wife was there, though by then in her eighties, and their younger son replied to the toast to his father's memory; and when the Centenary arrived in 1979, I found myself being interviewed by the BBC which broadcast, in all, seven reports on the most famous boys' magazine of them all.

Without Hutchison's devotion and his staff's loyalty and skill, I doubt if the paper would have survived the difficult years of the eighteen-nineties. A number of *B.O.P.*'s hopeful rivals had already died young, among them *The Union Jack*, which had been started, under Kingston's nominal editorship, when rumours of *B.O.P.* first got about. The writer G. A. Henty, later to contribute to *B.O.P.* himself, took it on for a short time. 'Henty bought it when it was in a bad way,' Gordon said laconically, 'woke it up for a time, and in his hands it died.' But new competitors kept appearing. In 1888 *B.O.P.* had bought up and absorbed Routledge's *Every Boy's Magazine*, and in 1894 Sampson Low's *Boys* was added. A strong competitor was *Chums*, first produced by Cassell's in 1892, with Max Pemberton as Editor. It made a poor start, but by 1900 had a good following in the public schools which were its principal market. Newnes' *The Captain* appeared in 1899 and appealed to youths with sophisticated tastes and the money to indulge them. Patrick Dunae calls it a 'slick periodical which catered to the more affluent'*. He praises its sports reporting, which was fuller and more up-to-date than *B.O.P.*'s; and its excellent fiction writers, who included P. G. Wodehouse and John Buchan, tempted away some readers. By October 3, 1899, the minutes speak of 'the serious decrease in the circulation of the *B.O.P.* and *G.O.P.*';

---

* Dunae, Patrick, *Boy's Own Paper: Origins and Editorial Policies*, The Private Library (journal of the Private Libraries Association), Second Series, Vol. 9, No. 4, Winter 1976.

six months later, of 'the falling off of the sale in *G.O.P.* and *B.O.P.* [which] is even larger than last year and demands serious attention.'

One of the measures adopted in the hope of bringing in more advertising revenue was the addition of wrappers to the weekly issues (decided at a meeting of the Finance Sub-Committee on September 16, 1897). However, *B.O.P.* stuck to its principles about the type of advertisements it could carry. Unlike *The Captain*, which had full-page cigarette advertising, *B.O.P.* steadfastly continued to sell its space to the makers of cricket bats, fishing rods, bicycle tyres and endless cocoa essences. Its advertisement revenue was always smaller than that of *G.O.P.*, which promoted an immense range of household goods for older readers—Vinolia Soap, sanitary towels, knitting machines and haberdashery, Beecham's pills, baking powder, blacklead polish and corsets.

Hutchison faced considerable problems in producing a quality magazine, on established lines, selling at only a penny a week. Despite the rising overheads, the question of increasing the price seems hardly to have been considered. The Finance Sub-Committee warned the magazine editors to be particularly stringent about the purchase of artwork. In

Above: some of the advertisements from the inside back cover of the Summer supplement, 1894

Drink CADBURY'S COCOA

ABSOLUTELY PURE, THEREFORE BEST.

" A Food alike suitable for building up the growing body and for repairing the waste which is incidental to all the processes of life."

HEALTH.

" A light, refreshing, and digestible beverage—absolutely pure Cocoa of the highest quality."—MEDICAL ANNUAL, 1890.

Above: whatever its rivals might do, B.O.P. remained faithful to its policy of advertising the nutritious and wholesome

July, 1897, to take one instance, it examined the purchase of illustrations for the Society's periodicals during the quarter April to June. The Editor of *Child's Companion*, *Little Dots*, and other RTS juvenile papers, who had spent £332 12s. 9d. on artwork, and had used only £140-worth, was called before the Committee to explain himself. During the same quarter, *G.O.P.* had spent £189 4s. 0d. and used £118-worth. *B.O.P.* must have been satisfactory for it alone was not mentioned; and at the close of the same year, Hutchison was singled out for particular praise. He and Peters were given an annual bonus calculated on the circulation rates of their respective papers. In November, Peters received £94 18s. 11d. for *G.O.P.* and Hutchison £31 4s. 4d. for *B.O.P.* But just a month later, the Sub-Committee awarded Hutchison £68 15s. 8d., 'in recognition of his care in purchasing illustrations for the *B.O.P.* and thereby preventing an accumulation of stock'. It was a once-in-a-lifetime gesture on their part.

By the turn of the century, the Religious Tract Society was also facing the problem of finding new premises. It eventually bought, in November 1902, 4 Bouverie Street, at the heart of the newspaper world (that fine writer, Ivor Brown, a *B.O.P.* contributor in my own day, described the Bouverie Street office to me as 'the most famous niche in Fleet Street') with all the usual attendant expense and upheaval.

By 1906, the sharp fall in sales had been arrested, but there was still a gradual decline. The paper remained popular and well regarded, it had a solid core of loyal subscribers throughout the Edwardian years, its readership was counted in hundreds of thousands, and yet its financial position grew ever weaker. The Society tried to cast its net more widely, unexpectedly producing in 1905 a new magazine of its own, under the title *Every Boy's Monthly*. It appeared on the fifteenth of each month, and was edited by Hutchison. Possibly the intention was to produce a paper devoted to hobbies, games and sports, outdoor interests and practical how-to-make-it features. Readers were urged to buy it as well as *B.O.P.*, but it can only have produced more overheads for *B.O.P.* itself.

In 1906 Charles Peters died, and the editorship of *G.O.P.* passed to Flora Klickmann, under whose aegis it was re-named *The Girl's Own Paper and Woman's Magazine*, in deference to its adult readership; the penny issues were discontinued, and the magazine became a sixpenny monthly. *B.O.P.*, however, struggled bravely on, with its penny weekly, its sixpenny monthly, and its familiar title. In August, 1909, the embattled Committee appointed a sub-committee to discuss the problem with Hutchison. As a result of their deliberations estimates were prepared for a revised *B.O.P.* 'more popular in character' ('Mr Hutchison is willing to consider its editorship') and for a new monthly magazine containing nothing but fiction. Neither plan was adopted, but the mere fact that both were seriously considered shows the degree to which the Committee was now prepared to compromise, and the severity of the situation facing the paper.

Hutchison was seventy before the Society decided to make him Consulting Editor and to appoint a younger man to the Editorship. Arthur Lincoln Haydon, the successful applicant, told me in 1954 how the post had been filled. When it was advertised, in 1912, there were over seven hundred applicants, including some women. Of these, about 550 had no experience of editing at all. They were schoolmasters or clergymen who plainly felt that producing a boys' magazine was child's play. Of the remaining 150, a couple of dozen were ex-Service, and their applications, too, were put aside—perhaps the Society felt that one Dr Stables was enough. This left 125 professional journalists, many of them elderly, of whom less than ten had any experience of voluntary work with young people. Bearing in mind the great success Charles Peters had made of *G.O.P.*, the Society looked for another Cassell's man. Their choice fell on Arthur Lincoln Haydon. He was a professional editor of forty-one, well-known in Fleet Street, and had done excellent work as sub-editor of the patriotic paper *Boys of Our Empire*. As a small boy of eight, he had trudged all the way up Highgate Hill to buy, from the newsagent at the top, a copy of the first issue of *B.O.P.*, and he had great regard for the paper. He accepted the appointment on June 11, 1912, and settled into the editorial office, with Hutchison at hand to advise, assist and warn.

Hutchison wanted to work to the end ('It is rest not rust I am after'), and his hope was fulfilled. He died on February 11, 1913, having been working at his desk as usual that morning. It was Gordon, for so long his right-hand man, who suggested that the family home at Leytonstone might be turned into a hostel, club and institute for boys, administered

An Important Announcement.

Above: a change-of-address notice to readers, published in the issue of October 3, 1903

The Son of an Anarchist.

A Tale of Strange
Mystery & Wild
Adventure,
by
W.A.B. CLEMENTSON,
M.A. Author of
'a Couple of Scamps,' etc.
CHAP. I.

"The boy was ready for him with another blow, and the drayman tottered." (See p. 258.)

Above: the first episode of a new serial published on January 25, 1913; schoolboy Ronald leaps to the defence of a little white-faced man being maltreated by a mob; and the crowd gives way. 'It is one thing to attack an alien and an anarchist, but to molest a healthy young Englishman was a more serious matter'

by the YMCA, in memory of Hutchison's great work. This practical and valuable idea had to be abandoned on the outbreak of the First World War the following summer, but in time Ivybank became a boys' home, and that would have made Hutchison very happy.

In my own time as Editor, *B.O.P.* readers were growing up in a world where social welfare was accepted as a commonplace. It was very different in Hutchison's day. He wanted to make his readers active doers of good, not passive spectators of the efforts of others. The causes that he and his team championed with such enthusiasm and practical support were many: Dr Barnardo's homes, ragged schools, orphanages, asylums and homes for working boys in London, training ships for the Merchant Navy, lifeboats for the RNLI, works schools in the great industrial firms (among them, Mather & Platts of Manchester, whose headmaster Don Davies, once a *B.O.P.* reader, later the magazine's leading sports contributor, was killed in the 'Manchester United' air crash at Munich in 1958). A *B.O.P.* bed in an East London hospital, a *B.O.P. Gordon Memorial* wing at the Barnardo Home for boys in Stepney, libraries for the London hospitals . . . all these and more were paid for with funds raised through the magazine.

The Committee wrote to Mrs Hutchison recording their great thankfulness for her husband's devoted work. 'The influence exerted through the *Boy's Own Paper*,' they said, 'covered not merely the leisure hours of its readers but often very deeply affected the spiritual and moral course of their whole lives.' They praised Hutchison's strong religious faith, his evangelical zeal, his insight into and sympathy with his readers. There was a chorus of agreement from churchmen, surgeons, academics, lawyers and headmasters. But perhaps the judgment of a fellow professional, written with the benefit of historical perspective fifty years later, would have given Hutchison particular pleasure. It described him as 'an ideal editor: unobtrusive, thorough, determined without dogmatism, and always alive and keen. Only those who know the inner workings of any sort of periodical can understand fully what such a character in the editor meant.'—thus F. J. Harvey Darton summed up Hutchison's achievement in *Children's Books in England*.

Under Hutchison, *B.O.P.*'s contributors included some of the most famous names in the land, but known or unknown, they were subordinate to the paper itself. The anonymity of many contributions served to heighten the effect. Like the *Manchester Guardian*, like *The Times*, like *Punch*, *B.O.P.* was a paper of character. Hutchison and his team had created a British institution.

Above and below left: two cartoons published in B.O.P. on April 25, 1903, and February 22, 1908, respectively, both carrying the same urgent message

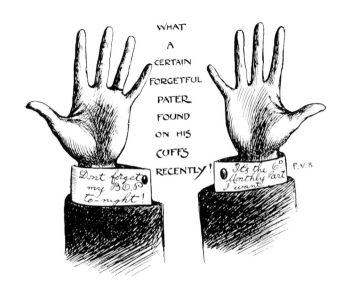

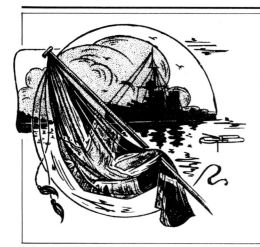

Chapter Eight

Mr A. L. Haydon, Editor

Arthur Lincoln Haydon was a professional to his fingertips. I knew him in the years after the Second World War, when I had taken over the editorship of *B.O.P.* Then in his eighties, he would travel from his home in Brighton to my office at 4 Bouverie Street, usually in the spring and summer months, every inch the Fleet Street editorial executive: light dapper clothes, a boldly contrasting spotted bow tie and pocket hand-kerchief to match, brightly polished lightweight shoes and—the Haydon touch at all seasons of the year—pale grey spats, to add a touch of sartorial excellence. 'I've always worn them!' he told me, laughing. 'In our game you need a few gimmicks and these are mine.'

In his early forties when he took over *B.O.P.*, Haydon was a youthful and vigorous man. Hutchison had never been robust, and had at one time invented a Fighting Editor to deal with would-be contributors who resented being turned down by this quiet, stocky, elderly man with spectacles and white beard. If an unwelcome caller appeared, Hutchison's staff tipped the wink to one of the packers, a massive man who was a sparring partner in his spare time, and he merely walked round the office breathing heavily ... This useful figure Haydon retained as long as possible.

Some of Haydon's descriptions of office practice at the time of his arrival fascinated me. He was astonished to find that all *B.O.P.* copy was filed in tea-chests. There was a chest for each week of the year, with the appropriate numeral in red paint on all four sides, plus chests for the monthly issues, the Summer and Christmas supplementaries, and the Annuals (each had its own particular colour of paint). Dozens of these chests had to be hauled on trolleys from desk to desk, some editorial staff being walled in by five or six at a time. They were all marked *B.O.P.* in bold capital letters, but this did not in fact stand for *Boy's Own Paper*, being a relic of the days when the tea-chests were full of Broken Orange Pekoe. Haydon introduced modern filing cabinets as soon as he could, though Gordon, loyal to his old chums, regretted the chests' departure.

Haydon soon learned that the Committee liked to take its time. His starting salary was to be revised after the first quarter. Three months

Above: a line decoration from Harry Wardale's poem, a Song of the Sea, *published in August, 1915*

came and went, and after a few weeks' silence, he applied for a revision; the Finance Sub-Committee considered it, pondered, and agreed (July, 1913) that 'no change should be made'. And that was that.

Taking on the editorship required a sense of vocation. In his own early days as G.O.P.'s editor, Charles Peters had apparently put in a similar request and got a cool reply ('A hope was expressed by the Committee that Mr Peters would act more in harmony with the principles of the Society,' ran a minute of July 20, 1882, deleted but still legible). When Dr Macaulay asked for a gratuity of £50 to cover editorial work on the two magazines in their early days, he was warned (July 15, 1886) that the arrangement was 'temporary and provisional' (it was to continue for nearly twenty years, at the Committee's wish) and he must not expect a permanent addition to his salary. Not a single request from Hutchison for a gratuity or salary increase was ever recorded. He had begun work on B.O.P. at a salary of £200, which was raised to £250 after the first year, with gratuities for the supplementary numbers and the Annuals (he usually got from £20 to £35; Peters got £50). In May, 1885, the irrepressible Peters applied to the Committee for a gratuity for the latest *Girl's Own Annual*, adding that he hoped 'a sum would be given him in some degree commensurate with the prosperity of the Periodical'; £75 was agreed. By June, 1887, Peters was making £400 salary, Hutchison £350, but the gratuities had at last stabilised at £50 each for the supplementaries, £100 each for the annuals, and in December, 1887, without request, discussion or comment in the minutes, Hutchison's salary too was raised to £400 a year.

No one who edited B.O.P. could hope to make a fortune, or indeed a substantial income. Haydon had to find other paid work to make ends meet. Fortunately, he could count on selling free-lance articles to Cassell's. In addition he was Honorary Secretary of the London Press Club during the First World War, though this was a labour of love.

Haydon soon recognised that instead of the monthly numbers supplementing sales of the weekly, as had been the case long ago in B.O.P.'s early days, the two issues had for years competed against one another; and in 1913 the decision to discontinue the weekly was at last made. B.O.P. became a 64-page, sixpenny monthly (eliminating 52 tea chests at a stroke!). One result of this was the need to choose serials with a strong story-line, characters and background bold enough to live in the mind for four weeks at a stretch, and neatly spaced climaxes tailored to keep the reader's interest going, month by month. During the first twelve-month, for instance, there were six. *The Heir of Wyselwood* (historical adventure at the time of the Napoleonic Wars) appeared in eight episodes, Jules Verne's *The Master of the World* in six, and *Under the Harrow* (a school story by the faithful B.O.P. writer John Lea) in four; all began in the November issue. *Under the Harrow* ended in February, and the strikingly titled *Peach Blossom's Peril*, another school tale, followed on in March. *The Master of the World* ended in April; in the same issue began *The Black Pearl of Peihoo*, a tale of the Malay Seas. A month later came the first episode of the *Adventures of Harry Leftwich*, another see-the-world story. *The Heir of Wyselwood* ended in June, and Peach Blossom emerged from peril in July, leaving *The Black Pearl* and *Harry Leftwich* to run on

Above: Arthur Lincoln Haydon in his later years. He took over the editorship of B.O.P. *in the summer of 1912, when he was in his early forties, and remained until 1924. It thus fell to him to guide the paper through the years of the First World War*

OUR PRIZE COMPETITION AWARDS.

" B.O.P."
Cricket
Competition.

(See page 496 for details.)

No. 1.—A Mixed Team of British and Australians to Play the World.

THE following are the names of the chosen team, in order of votes received :

Rhodes, Trumper, Fry, Hirst, Noble, Lilley, Maclaren, Trumble, Ranjitsinhji, Hill, Foster.

The prize has been won by C. H. SEATON, 4 Queenswood Avenue, Highgate, N., whose list contained all the above names.

The lists of 57 competitors contained ten of the selected team ; and then those of others tailed off to three or four names only. 376 readers took part in this competition.

P.V.B.

Above: Hutchison faced with entries for a B.O.P. competition (1904)

Far right: written by J. Claverdon Wood, and illustrated by Arthur Twidle, superb practitioners both, Jeffrey of the White Wolf Trail *ran from October 7, 1911, to February 10, 1912 (Volume XXXIV) and carried its young hero to the New World. There he was befriended by the Pawnee, hunted by the Sioux, tried cattle ranching, was captured by horse-thieves, mined for silver, and eventually made his fortune—but 'what is gold to a man whose ambitions did not soar beyond an Indian wigwam, and whose best possessions were health, a rifle, a dog, a horse, and a friend?'*

in harness until October. In addition there were 31 'complete' stories, only two of which over-ran into a second issue. Regular items were the usual mix of practical and informative features, correspondence, the *B.O.P. Gardener* series, notes about the *B.O.P. League of Friendship*, *Our Note Book* (anecdotes and snippets of information), sports features, articles, poems, puzzles and problems, and *In Lighter Mood*—a page of humorous stories with contributions from readers who competed for the best funny story.

The idea of competitions had been fostered by Hutchison in the early days, when entrants were divided into three classes: under sixteen, sixteen to nineteen, and nineteen to twenty-three. By the Edwardian period the age limits had disappeared. Considering the fact that *B.O.P.* had an international reputation, and many older readers, I am surprised by the modest nature of the prizes—under £3 *in all* for a 'Go As You Please' competition in 1905. Whenever *B.O.P* ran a make-a-model competition of this kind, entries flooded into the office; unpacking them, judging them, repacking and returning them to readers who had sent the return postage, disposing of the others—it must have taken hours. A seventeen-year-old girl reader, Violet Bettinson of Lincoln, won first prize, ten shillings and sixpence, (52½p), for a Naples fruit stall made from cigar boxes. Her older sister Nina came second. After them came the boys: G. S. Phillpott of Nottingham, aged sixteen, with a model newsagent's shop (*B.O.P.* prominently on display); A. L. Smith of Southport, a fourteen-year-old stripling, with a model Swiss chalet; and F. E. Gower of North London, no less than twenty-five, with a bent-iron rose-bowl. Hutchison sternly warned his readers that the purchase of a single copy did not entitle a whole family—or indeed a whole school— to compete. 'We have stated this many times.' Why did he not introduce a simple competition entry form or coupon?

In his first year Haydon kept to competitions producing entries which were rather easier to handle (the best photographs on a set subject, the best answers to a series of questions on the laws of cricket, the best story for 'a picture wanting words'). The outbreak of the First World War in the summer of 1914 reduced the range still further; the funny story competition remained, but there was only one other competition, for the best naval or military photograph. Total prize money, £3 11s 0d for British readers, and a further £1 16s 6d for Colonial competitors, for whom the entry date was extended.

I myself found competitions an excellent way of encouraging boys to play some part in running the paper, and remember one blank-verse letter which we published in 1953, Coronation Year, from a reader named Julian Cooper:

I have three hats
And not one of them belongs to me properly.
There is my grandfather's Homburg,
Which I use for hay-making.
There is a Portuguese straw hat
Left behind by a German in Poitiers,
And there is a felt hat of medium quality
Given to me by a man on Cambridge station.

JEFFREY OF THE WHITE WOLF TRAIL.

By J. CLAVERDON WOOD,

Author of "Sinclair of the Scouts."

(Illustrated by ARTHUR TWIDLE.)

CHAPTER I.—"A DIFFICULT CASE."

JACK JEFFREY sat in the little private room which was solemnly set aside by Dr. Melldon for purposes of correction with a considerable amount of anxious foreboding. He had been summoned from the playground by the Senior Prefect, Teddy Rutherford, and knew that something out of the ordinary had happened.

"It's a jolly big row this time, Jeff," said Rutherford, with a grin; "the Chief has got his danger-signal up and looks like a mad bull. Marshall, the gipsy, has been with him for the last hour or so, and the landlord of the King's Head has just gone into the Chamber of Horrors too. What in the world have you been up to?"

"Racing," replied Jack, with a shrug of his shoulders. "I won the Hunt Cup on that big horse which belongs to Marshall's crowd. No one else could ride the brute, and they gave me no peace until I promised to do what I could. I called myself Smith, but some fellow must have blabbed. I knew it was a silly thing to do, but I am a perfect fool where horses are concerned, and when Marshall pressed me to ride the big horse I could not say 'No.' I expect I shall be expelled. Old Melldon will never forgive this last exploit. He hates horses and racing almost as much as he detests gipsies and publicans. It's just my wretched luck!"

Jeffrey had not to wait very long before the Doctor came bustling into the room. Taking two or three paces up and down and muttering and frowning, the schoolmaster suddenly stopped before the lad. His face was red with anger. With a great effort he controlled himself.

"Well, sir," he said at length, "what have you to say concerning this last discreditable business, which is a disgrace to my school? You have now reached the end of my patience and forbearance. But this is only on a par with your usual behaviour. You have been under my charge for the past eight years, and I assure you that you have given me more anxiety than any other boy I have ever known.

"You have ability which you have never used. Your favourite companions have been gamekeepers, poachers, and gipsies, tavern-haunters, whose vile pursuits you have followed rather than those of gentlemen. Every low boxer within twenty miles of the school knows about you, and the county justices would have prosecuted you for poaching if it had not been for the disgrace which would have fallen upon me. But I never dreamed that you would figure upon a racecourse and as the rider of a vicious brute which belongs to a set of gipsy marauders. Marshall is a fit companion for a lad of your disposition. Let me tell you that I am not going to put up with any more wickedness of this description. Before

your father died in India he entrusted his motherless lad to my care. I wish I had known a little more about him. I know that his relatives rightly cast him off after he had married your mother, but——"

The lad started to his feet with a crimsoned face. "Excuse me, sir," he said, with an ugly glint in his eyes, "you will be wise to keep off that topic. I never allow anyone to discuss my mother. My father was a soldier and a man of honour, and when he married my mother it was his own concern. She was a farmer's daughter and he was a baronet's youngest son, but I'm not going to let you or anybody else say a word to her discredit. If my father's people cast him off, that was their concern and their loss. So drop it, sir, or there will be more trouble than you reckon upon."

Dr. Melldon bit his lips and looked at the lad in silence. He was a schoolmaster of the old type, over-inclined to severity, but he felt that he had gone too far in touching upon the boy's mother. He returned to the subject of the race-

"'Excuse me, sir,' he said, with an ugly glint in his eyes."

course, and wisely said no more upon the forbidden topic. He had right upon his side when he said that escapades of this description could not be allowed. Every public-house in the district had made a hero of the lad whose courage and skill had guided the big horse to victory, and the incidents in his career had been retailed with infinite gusto and exaggeration.

Everything the Doctor had said about the pursuits

of Jeffrey was perfectly true. The lad had always shown a distaste for quiet studies and scholarship, and had devoted his leisure time to exercises which were detestable in the eyes of a man like Dr. Melldon. He had delighted in swimming, boxing, hunting, and riding, and during the past five years he had made himself the talk of the neighbourhood. On more than one occasion he had narrowly escaped arrest for poaching, although it was admitted that his interest lay more in the snaring of game than in the carrying of it off.

He had climbed out of his dormitory window one holiday time and disappeared for more than three weeks. When he returned he confessed that he had stowed himself away on a coasting brig and gone cruising along the French and Spanish coasts. On another occasion, at Christmas-time, he had vanished from the dreary, almost empty school, and tramped to the Midlands in order to face a boasting iron-worker in Tipton, and the form-master had afterwards discovered in his dormitory a newspaper

This amusing little letter somehow caught the imagination of *B.O.P.* readers in that carefree summer. Before long we were receiving hundreds of letters from readers telling us about hats they too wore but did not properly own. We treated it as a competition, and it linked readers from all over the world. Robin Lamplough of Eastnor, then in Southern Rhodesia, with a khaki hat, once his grandfather's, worn in the Zulu Wars in 1879, the year *B.O.P.* was founded, with a bullet hole in the brim. Fred Harper of Iver, Bucks, fielding at a comic cricket match, in a straw hat with his sister's shorn plaits attached. And A. Weaver of Peterborough, cheering frantically at Murrayfield as Scotland took on the mighty All-Blacks, when a shiny black sou'wester dropped out of the air as an original and useful memento of the day. We paid fifteen shillings (75p) for every letter we published. Space fillers like this are a boon to editors.

The competition lists produce many surprises. I remember an occasion when the names and addresses of two readers from my home town in Lancashire caught my eye, in an issue published sixty-five years earlier. I found that I had known their homes well as a boy—spacious Manchester cotton-merchant houses set in beautiful grounds with peacocks on guard. *B.O.P.* links are very sound. And I remember too finding *J. L. Garvin (16), Birkenhead, Cheshire* among the prize-winners in a literary competition, in 1884. Was this the start of a long and distinguished career, culminating in his becoming editor of *The Observer*? That same morning I discovered that Gustav Theodore Holst, an Essex schoolboy of Swedish descent, had won a *B.O.P.* musical competition. (Later he became a contributor as well.) Here was a British composer of outstanding musical gifts. The young Edwin Lutyens was another *B.O.P.* reader who won a book prize in one of the competitions, and kept it all his life.

Of *B.O.P.*'s features in Haydon's time, *In Lighter Mood* has probably suffered most from the passing of time; anecdotal humour tends to date very quickly. One- and two-liners last better, and their very hoariness adds to their appeal for young readers. In the mid-nineteen-fifties we ran a 'gag bag' feature, under the by-lines of famous comedians, many of whom are still happily entertaining audiences today. Benny Hill, Harry Secombe, Jimmy Edwards, Terry-Thomas, Charlie Chester, Tommy Trinder; Arthur Askey, who remembered doing his piano practice as a boy with *B.O.P.* propped on the rack in place of his music; and the splendid conjuror David Nixon, who told us that as a boy he had sent in joke after joke, but never won a *B.O.P.* prize. Bob Monkhouse, too, was interviewed for *B.O.P.* and told our reporter Herbert Harris (February, 1955) that in his schooldays he drew and sold cartoon strips for magazines. 'I once burned the midnight oil doing some drawings for *B.O.P.*— something really special, because they said *B.O.P.* required such a high standard—but I finally tore the things up.' Eric Barker, too (whose father's firm, Aylott and Barker, supplied the paper on which the magazine was printed) sent in a contribution as a boy, and had it gently returned by the Editor of the day; but his was a full-length school story, carrying on the tradition begun by T. B. Reed, and nurtured by every editor from Hutchison onwards, until my own time, after the Second World War, when its appeal at last declined.

FOR ENGLAND AND THE RIGHT!

A Tale of the War in Belgium.

 By A. L. HAYDON,

Author of "The Book of the V.C.," "With Pizarro the Conquistador," etc.

It was fortunate for Haydon that the change from a weekly to a monthly had been accomplished before the outbreak of war in August, 1914. He held the price at sixpence until November 1916, when it rose by a penny; wartime shortages compelled him to raise it again, first to eightpence, then ninepence, and at last, in 1918, to one shilling. He had been instructed to keep the *Boy's Own Annual* going at all costs and told that any way in which *B.O.P.* could help the national war effort should be encouraged. A decade earlier, during the Boer War, three of the Society's supporters had complained about the 'inflammatory and war-like character of *B.O.P.*', meeting with a vigorous rebuttal from the Committee, which added: 'The Editor's conduct in keeping out of his pages all that could influence the minds of his readers entailed heavy loss on the Society.' The first *B.O.P.* serial of them all, *From Powder Monkey to Admiral*, written by Kingston, revised by Hutchison, had also been criticised as being too militaristic and 'encouraging warlike spirit'. To this charge Kingston replied with dignity, saying that although his story did indeed show scenes of naval warfare in the Napoleonic wars, it never belittled the horrors of battle, or allowed boys to fancy war 'a glorious thing'; and it encouraged the belief that the victor should be magnanimous and merciful to 'enemies in distress'.

Now, however, the full weight of the paper's influence was given to encouraging the war effort, and this was in tune with Haydon's own convictions. With his years on the patriotic journal *Boys of Our Empire* at his back, he relished the task of coping with the stresses of wartime publishing. The new Volume, XXXVII, opened that November with two 'peacetime' serials, which had been already on the stocks before the

Above: in November, 1914, three months after the outbreak of the First World War, B.O.P. published a topical serial, written against time by its Editor (Volume XXXVII)

outbreak of war; *In the Power of the Pygmies: A Tale of the Great African Forest* was one, by a favourite author, Captain Charles Gilson, and the other was *Beyond the School Gates: A Story of School and City Life* by Paul Blake (H. M. Paull). With them, however, Haydon managed to bring in a timely short story by Ernest Richards (*The Wander Vogel: A Tale of a German Spy*) and an article on The Royal Flying Corps—'Until the present war is over no further recruiting for the Corps is taking place' this said, with an 'over-by-Christmas' confidence. In his editorial, Haydon urged his readers to support the Boy Scouts, join the rifle clubs and cadet corps, practise drill and athletics, keep themselves healthy, play their part. Meanwhile, Haydon himself was writing at full speed *For England and the Right! A Tale of the War in Belgium* which began in January, 1915. Foreseeing the shortage of topical fiction, he also contributed short stories under the name of 'Lincoln Hayward', among them *The Mystery of the Loch: A Story of the Great War*. Though predictable in content (a German U-boat nosing among lonely lochs to seek out a

Below: The Smart Set *by Michael Dorani, a complete short story with a public-school setting, appeared in May, 1915 (Volume XXXVII)*

The Smart Set.

A Public School Story.

By MICHAEL DORANI.

I.

THE Captain of Stonehurst College opened his study door and looked down the passage.

"Fa-ag!" he shouted, as no one was in sight.

There was no answering patter of feet, and he called again—somewhat louder. This time a door opened somewhere below, and a cheerful-looking youngster, with fiery-red hair, came running up the stairs.

"Yes, Graham!" he said breathlessly; "do you want me?"

"Well, I believe I do," said the Captain dryly. "Just send Stewart up here, will you? Oh, and you'd better tell Harrison and Fisher to come with him."

The fag departed on his errand, and the senior entered his study, where he sat musing in an arm-chair before the fire. About five minutes had elapsed when there was a knock at the door.

"Come in!" cried Graham, rising to meet the visitors; and they obeyed the behest. "Ah, how d'you do, Stewart! I see you've brought the 'Co.' along with you. That's good, we'll be able to get to work quicker. Make yourselves comfortable, boys; I'm not going to give you a 'wigging.'"

Stewart & Co. grinned, and seated themselves round the fire, while the Captain rummaged in a cupboard, and produced three glasses and a bottle of lime-juice.

"I want you to do me a job," he announced, filling the glasses and handing them round. "It will take up most of your spare time; but you won't mind that when I explain. It concerns the honour of the school deeply, and I know you'd do anything to save the old place from degradation."

"Ra-a-ther!" was the emphatic response.

Graham nodded, and, after carefully locking the door and placing the key in his pocket, seated himself in the arm-chair.

"I'd better explain, first of all, what you have to pit your wits against," he began in a low voice. "There's a set of silly young bounders in the school—the majority of whom are in the Shell form—who think it's clever, and 'doggish,' to go out playing cards at a beastly low saloon in the village. They smoke cheap cigarettes, gamble on the turf, and hob-nob with all the riff-raff of the country-side. Now, that spells only one word for fellows of their age and experience—*ruin!*"

His listeners' faces were very concerned as he stopped and looked at them.

"Oh!" murmured Fisher. "I thought our fellows were all above that sort of thing!"

"So did I," returned the Captain grimly, "till I was told of it by another prefect who left last term. He didn't know their names, and I've been trying to find them out from the beginning of the term. As you see, I have had no success. Well, it struck me just now that if you were to take up the trail, you might have more chance; the fellows wouldn't be likely to suspect you, and you can go among them—especially the Shell fellows—more than I can, as I have a lot of other things to see to. What do you say?"

"We'd be awfully glad to do it, Graham, but——" Stewart halted awkwardly, and the Captain smiled.

"I know what you're thinking," he said coolly. "You

'An Average Bit of a Briton.'

Words by J. W. E.   A SONG FOR BOYS.   Music by J. H. F.

Above: a characteristic wartime song which was published in the issue of May, 1918 (Volume XL)

suitable fuel dump), this had the right wartime touch and hint of spies, dismissed as soon as mentioned. Captain Gilson weighed in with *At the Call of the Tsar: A Tale of the First Russian Advance* (1916–17). The first two episodes are set in an English public school, complete with an idolised Second Prefect, a crafty but redeemable bully, the theft of some treasured postage stamps, a new boy falsely accused, a schoolboy feud, and the winning of the inter-House cricket cup. At the close of the second instalment the strange new senior, Irben, reveals his identity to his friend Rashleigh. He is the young Grand Duke of a Baltic state, soon to be summoned home to his regiment. Rashleigh is deeply envious ('Fancy taking part in a war! Better than a house match!') and joyfully wins parental permission to accompany him. The remainder of the story is taken up by their exploits against the Prussians, and in particular their foiling of plans laid by the master spy. Long, rambling, but none the less well-written school stories were still much favoured for wartime reading. The search for a new Talbot Baines Reed produced no true successor, but Haydon did his best with John Lea, on the writing staff since 1894, and Kent Carr, whose serial *The Shaping of Jephson's: A Story of Public School Life* appeared in 1916–17. 'Kent Carr' was the pseudonym of Gertrude Kent Oliver, one of *B.O.P.*'s lady contributors, most of whom discreetly concealed their identity under *noms de plume* or initials. J. Claverdon Wood, Argyll Saxby, Harold Avery, Godfray Sellick: all contributed fine energetic adventure stories in the *B.O.P.* tradition, throughout the Haydon years.

Haydon's wartime editorials described the exploits of Service heroes and recorded the names of *B.O.P.* casualties. It is sad to come upon a familiar name, 'Captain Talbot Reed of the 67th Punjabis' ('Tibbie'

How Private Lauder of the Royal Scots Fusiliers won the V.C.

Reed's younger son), killed in action. A new feature began, *War Notes and Pictures*—brief items and anecdotes about equipment and tactics. The magazine published rousing wartime songs (*An Average Bit of a Briton*); poems, many of which linked service at the Front to the discipline learned in schooldays (*For the Honour of the School, To the Old Boys at the War, A Recruit, The Old School's Roll of Honour, School and War*); articles encouraging readers to do their bit towards improving the nation's food supplies by keeping goats, pigs, poultry, rabbits, pigeons and bees, and by collecting wild berries, acorns, chestnuts and nettles as foodstuffs; and the usual advice on caring for pets—caged birds seem to have been particularly popular at this time, and *B.O.P.* handed out advice for asthmatic canaries (paint all crevices in the cage with fir-tree oil) and similar problems. Haydon kept up the Baden-Powell connection, especially in the war years, with items such as *Boy Scouts and the War, Chinese Boy Scouts*, and *A Royal Boy Scout*—the latter being the eleven-year-old Prince of the Asturias, eldest son of the King of Spain, photographed in full uniform with drill shirt, leather belt, well-cut corduroy shorts (the Royal knees are clearly visible), water-bottle, knapsack, neatly folded cloak-blanket over his shoulder, the old familiar broad-brimmed Baden-Powell Scout hat in his left hand, and the Scout staff, 'invaluable for warding off mad dogs as well as building stretchers and bridges' in his right, held at the Alert position.

Haydon also made the most of the famous *B.O.P.* presentation plates. In 1913-14, the presentations ranged from *Football Colours of Our Public Schools* by V. Wheeler Holohan to *A Very Gallant Gentleman* by J. C. Dollman, a sepia reproduction of a Royal Academy exhibit, showing Captain Oates going out to die in the Antarctic blizzard. With the outbreak of war came *Regiments of British Yeomanry, Past and Present, 1794-1914*; *Sons of the Brave* (a painting by Phil Morris, with a cadet corps marching forth in scarlet and gold, while widows and children looked proudly on); *Flags of All Nations*; '*The Whole Line will Advance!*' by Edgar A. Holloway (Wellington at Waterloo); and the Prince of Wales in the uniform of the Grenadier Guards. '*Well Passed, Sir!*', in sepia (Ernest Prater) kept up the sporting interest; while for the natural historians there were *The Destroyers* by C. E. Swan (a leopard and a snake) and *Birds of Paradise*, painted especially for *B.O.P.* by a favourite artist, Arthur Twidle, who had illustrated several of J. Claverdon Wood's *B.O.P.* serials. The *B.O.P. Portrait Gallery* in Volume XXXIX, 1916-17, opened

Below: Dumb Heroes at the Front, *a fine drawing by Stanley L. Wood which showed an artillery train taking up its position under fire, was published in October, 1917 (Volume XL)*

Who will leave the town now,
Who will follow me
Out into the green fields far?
Throw the dull book down now,
Spring is on the tree,
All where the white tents are.

Who will keep behind now,
Who's the man to stay
Lone in the sombre street?
Magic's in the wind now,
Sunlight all the way,
Wings on the joyful feet.

No, no! for the rare bells
Are calling full loud,
Unheard when the boy's heart's old,
Windbells, harebells,
Music of cloud,
Song that the green trees hold.

Here's a road to follow,
A white road and long,
Deep into the singing noon.
Springtime and swallow,
Springtime and song,
Daylight, starlight, moon!

Here where grass and loam be,
Wood and meadow scents,
All things that God first grew.
Here shall our house be,
Under the white tents,
Here where the old world's new.

with a photograph of Alfred Pearse, who had by then given close on forty years' loyal service. It included the naturalist George Soper; Claverdon Wood in yachtsman's oilskins; Captain Gilson in khaki; Stanley Wood, an immensely popular *B.O.P.* artist, the first illustrator of Cutliffe Hyne's 'Captain Kettle' tales; and *B.O.P.*'s senior contributor—the indefatigable Gordon.

In 1920, when the struggles of the war lay safely in the past, Gordon began to think of retiring. He was then seventy-two, and was in fact to stay at his post for a further thirteen years. Haydon brought his only son into the office, to train as a sub-editor, but alas, the boy died of TB in his early twenties. The loss hit Haydon very hard. He was never quite the same man again.

Haydon was, in any case, becoming irked by the Society's insistence on supervising his professional duties. Unlike the evangelical Hutchison, to whom it was all in the day's work, he had never taken kindly to watchful 'clerics' (his name for the Society staff), and after ten years' service, he felt he could be trusted to check and sign the master page proof and send it to the printer on his own authority. Instead, once a month, he had to take the proof by hand by Croydon, to be considered by 'a retired bishop'. Here the proof was carried off upstairs by an intermediary, and Haydon was left to cool his heels in an anteroom, with tea, biscuits, and a copy of the *Times*. He waited two or three hours, sometimes longer, before the intermediary re-appeared with the proof, rarely if ever touched by the higher authority aloft.

In the autumn of 1924 Haydon left *B.O.P.* He also gave up the editorship of the new weekly magazine for Scouts, *Rovering*, which he had introduced earlier that year (it did not long survive his departure). He joined the London School of Journalism as a Senior Tutor, a fitting post for a man of his experience and gifts. He had always loved words—their history, their meanings—and had a strong feeling for sentence structure. Eric Partridge, his friend and colleague, dedicated to him a definitive work on punctuation, and in his spare time he wrote concise definitions for *Nuttall's Dictionary*, almost his only specific hobby—though he could talk, and talk well, on virtually any subject. His professional contacts in Fleet Street had been of great benefit to *B.O.P.*, as had his eye for talent. One of his last discoveries for the paper was a young Manchester poet, Louis Golding, who contributed *Route-Marching Song* in May, 1924, and *Camping Song* a year later. Louis was to become a best-selling novelist, with his stories of Jewish life in Manchester. He had a marked affection for *B.O.P.*, and during my own time as Editor I had the pleasure of attending his wedding reception at the Café Royal. Louis was then sixty-three, and the literary world turned out *en masse* to celebrate an event it had never expected to see. I found myself sitting beside J. B. Priestley, who was delightful. 'I'd have written for the *B.O.P.* if anyone had ever asked me,' he said—but added, like a true Yorkshireman, 'but I'd have wanted a bit more than a guinea a page.' What would Haydon have thought of the one that got away?

Chapter Nine
MrG.R.Pocklington, Editor

Geoffrey Richard Pocklington accepted the editorship in December 1924. He was the only bachelor to edit *B.O.P.* Educated at Rossall and Balliol, he made his home in Suffolk, and was in comfortable circumstances. Fleet Street, which liked him, spoke of him as 'an honorary gent', and he often signed himself 'Hon. Editor', so he may not have drawn a salary. Like Haydon, he was a devoted supporter and benefactor of the Scout Association, and served as District Scout Commissioner for his beautiful village home, Chelsworth, and its district, for many years. He was a reticent man, modest and self-effacing to a degree, but well-liked, meticulous and thorough.

Pocklington inherited a 72-page one-shilling monthly. It was printed on good paper and cleanly produced, but there was little money to spare. Authors were paid quarterly, after publication, and at modest terms, so that few 'big names' were attracted. None the less, *B.O.P.* managed to survive the terrifying depression between the wars. Two of its old competitors sank out of sight, *The Captain* failing in 1925 and *Chums* in 1933, but there were others on the scene, notably the weekly paper *The Scout* and the respected *Children's Newspaper*.

Pocklington's first editorial appeared in March, 1925. He spoke to his readers in the first person, telling them that he had been brought up on *B.O.P.* as a schoolboy; but whereas Haydon had signed each editorial 'A.L.H.', Pocklington wrote simply and anonymously 'The Editor'. He asked readers to let him have their suggestions for improving the paper, and on his own account said that he felt the heavy proportion of prizes to entries in the competitions should be reduced—'To win a prize in a *B.O.P.* competition ought to be something of a distinction, and not merely a chance of adding another book to your shelves.' Haydon had taken a different view, wishing to give his readers a good chance of winning *something*, and recent prize competitions had offered a camera, pen, paintbox and the like as first prizes, postal orders for second and third, and 250 volumes a month for runners-up.

The response to Pocklington's invitation was varied, as might have

Above: a line decoration from December 21, 1912 (Volume XXXV)

THE EDITOR'S PAGE

Above: the decorative heading for Pocklington's editorials showed him, characteristically, with a gathering of readers from all over the world. The B.O.P.'s League of Friendship *was particularly close to his heart*

been expected. Some readers wanted him to abolish the stamp column altogether, others urged him to give it more space; and so on. But on one point the great majority was in agreement: 'The serial story is not so popular as it used to be.' Readers said, first and foremost, that a month between episodes was a long time to wait, and secondly, that 'when a fellow happens to have a spare shilling to spend on a *B.O.P.* he likes to have a number complete in itself and not one with the middles of several stories, of which he has not read the beginning and may not be able to read the end'. Pocklington saw the force of this, accepting that many boys simply could not afford to subscribe regularly. In October, 1925, *B.O.P.* began its forty-eighth year, and the handling of the serials was changed. Each was to be completed in two, or at the most three, long instalments, the second and third opening with a synopsis of what had gone before, and as a general rule only one serial was to appear in any issue.

The first issue set the pattern. It contained the first 20-page episode of *Troop One of the Labrador*, a Scouting story set in Canada, by Dillon Wallace, which was concluded in the following month; a short historical adventure by May Wynne, *Count Deither's Mousetrap* ('How now, Heinrich? Hath misfortune chanced yonder?'); a time-slip adventure in Peru (*The Lake of the Sacrifice* by B. Thorburn-Clarke); *His Chance* by Francis H. Sibson (naval heroism in 1,500 words); and *The School House Mascot* by the much-loved Harold Avery, who had been writing for *B.O.P.* for over a quarter of a century. Supplementing the fiction were articles on *The Boy's Own Wireless Set*, *Ancient Bridges*, *Block Printing for Boys*, *How to Make an Electric Motor*, *Sailors in the Making* and *The Boyhood of Nelson*, and the *Art of Handling Wild Animals*; two sets of narrative verses and

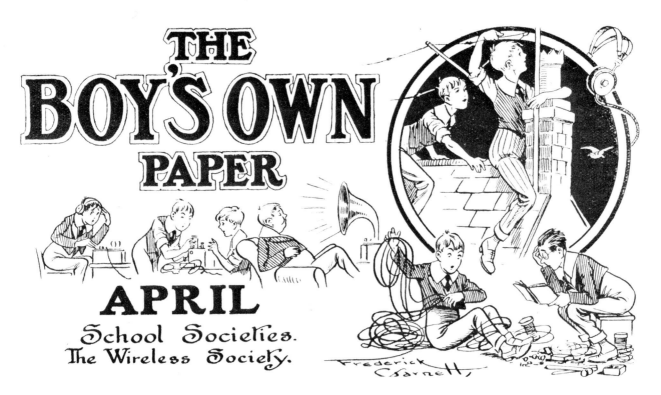

THE BOY'S OWN PAPER

APRIL

School Societies.
The Wireless Society.

Frederick Garnett

Above: one of the twelve decorative mastheads of Volume XLVII (1924–5), all drawn by Frederick Garnett; these featured a series of twelve school societies typical of the time—Music, Astronomy, Drama, Debates, Chess, Model Engineering, Wireless, Photography, Natural History, Rambling, Philately and Glee-Singing

two short poems; a full-page monochrome presentation plate of the Prince of Wales; half a dozen regular features—the *Boy's Own Coin Corner*, *Notes from Overseas*, the *Boy's Own Field Club*, *Correspondence*, and the *Editor's Page*. No sport—but that was put right in the following month, with *Hints for Rugger Players*; a full-colour fold-out presentation plate of *Some Football Colours of Our Public Schools*; *Football Songs of the Public Schools*; and *The Rugger Match* (a full-page poem). The regular *Chess Corner* also appeared. Christmas brought pantomimes and amateur dramatics, 'paper cricket', and conjuring tricks. With the New Year in January came *Scout Craft*, a play for boys; the first of a series of articles on scouting at the public schools; *How Scouting Began* by Baden-Powell himself, with a full-page presentation portrait, just right for the Scout Hut; and a short story about scouting, *His Royal Highness* by Edmund Burton. Pocklington liked to use a theme, where possible, to shape and colour a particular issue.

He dropped the humorous page, *In Lighter Mood*, feeling that it had become a ragbag of very ancient jokes. But his readers regretted its loss and in October 1927, true to his principles, Pocklington restored it at their particular wish. He stressed that jokes 'on sacred subjects, or intoxication, or involving the use of bad language are not wanted and will not be accepted', and he retitled the feature, wryly, *Under the Spreading Chestnut Tree*. The mild-mannered jokes proved so popular that it was still a regular feature long after Pocklington's departure, and re-appeared in my own early years as Editor.

In 1927 Pocklington introduced the *B.O.P. Club*, a cause dear to his heart, which brought together the *League of Friendship* founded in 1912, in the last days of Hutchison's editorship (a loose-knit association of

THE SECOND BEST.

I.

You ask me for a toast to-night
  In this familiar hall,
Where well-known objects greet the sight
  And boyhood's days recall.

II.

Some honoured name, I think you said,
  But what have I to say?
The King, the Services, the Head,
  The Heroes of the Day.

III.

To each with joyous shouts and pride
  Has loud acclaim been paid:
Forgive me if I turn aside
  From sunshine into shade.

IV.

For now a shadow throng I see
  From seats long vacant rise,
A faint reproach there seems to be
  In their world-weary eyes.

V.

Their voices cross our song and jest
  From camp and field and town,
The men who did their level best
  Yet never won renown.

VI.

Amongst the nameless dead they lie
  In unrecorded graves,
And o'er their memory roll high
  The world's oblivious waves.

VII.

Yet though the school they loved so well
  No more records their name;
Though on their brows there may not dwell
  A crown of earthly fame;

VIII.

Though on life's battlefield their part
  Was not to gain the prize;
Still deep in some old comrade's heart
  Enshrined their memory lies.

IX.

The steadfast hearts that never quailed,
  The tongues that never lied,
The faithful hands that never failed—
  No longer at my side.

X.

I give to-night no foremost name,
  I give no honoured guest:
I think of those unknown to fame
  And give—"The Second Best."
              H. ELRINGTON.

Above: a poem by H. Elrington, published in B.O.P. on February 5, 1910 (Volume XXXII)

readers sharing a common ideal but bound by no formal promises) and the *Boy's Own Field Club* founded by Haydon in 1915. He took a particular interest in the Pen Friends Scheme, linking *B.O.P.* readers of similar ages and interests throughout the world. Parents, teachers, youth leaders and clergy approved and encouraged the scheme. It cost virtually nothing to operate but it cemented goodwill between *B.O.P.* readers in more than forty countries. Many of these postal friendships survived the Second World War, and during my own time as Editor (1946-66) I came across *B.O.P.* readers, put in touch with one another by Pocklington, who had continued to correspond for thirty years or more.

As many of his answers to correspondents show, Pocklington was a man of great, quiet kindness. He went out of his way to help readers with educational worries—such as the supply of second-hand school text-books—and gave careful advice on careers and openings in commerce and industry. He urged readers to consider working in 'the vast open spaces of the great Overseas Dominions, scarcely peopled as yet, and crying out for boys and men of the right type to come and develop their wonderful natural resources' and in this cause introduced to *B.O.P.* the Imperial Migration Bureau, whose Commissioner would inform, advise and assist boys who were genuinely interested in making a career overseas.

I never met Pocklington, although I wanted to do so, and almost succeeded during the Whitsun holiday of 1950. My wife and I were staying with the Geoffrey Morgans at Bildeston, only a couple of miles from Chelsworth. I made an appointment to call, but he was elderly by then, and very ill, and could not after all see me. He died soon after. But my own schooldays covered the years 1926 to 1934, so I saw the Pocklington epoch at first hand.

It was a time when family resources were strained to the utmost by the aftermath of the First World War, ex-servicemen suffering disabilities of all kinds, vast long-term unemployment and the untold horrors that went with it, and illness prevalent among women whose courage and willpower were stretched to the absolute limits of endurance. My contemporaries and I longed to find some way of making ourselves less of a burden on the family finances. On my way to and from school I used to pass a newsagent's shop and one rainy Wednesday in the spring of 1927, saw a notice in the window. It said, very simply: *Strong Lad Required to Help with Morning and Evening Paper Deliveries. Apply Within.*

I applied within at once and was surveyed up and down, and from all angles, by a canny Lancashire family who were taking no chances. Yes, they thought I could do the job. When could I start? 'Tomorrow,' I said without thinking. 'Right then, lad, tomorrow will do us. Be here sharp at 6.50 a.m. You are not allowed on the streets before seven or after eight in the morning. In the evenings we will need you at the station at 5.15 p.m. to help carry the papers to the shop. Then there's a shorter round from just before six until half-past or so. Six days a week we'll need you. The pay is four shillings a week, paid on Friday nights.' Four shillings was twenty new pence a week, a fortune in those days. *Four shillings!* FOUR SHILLINGS!

I went home and told my mother, who cried. I told my father, a disabled war pensioner, who disapproved. But off I went the next morning, and I found I quite liked the job. On the following day, Friday, the weight seemed enormous because it was the day our local paper came out and everybody took that as well as their usual paper. I did not expect any money that week as I had only done three days, but on Saturday evening the newsagent stopped me as I was going home. 'We are pleased with you, lad,' he said, 'here's something for this week.' He gave me a brand-new half-crown. I was so thrilled, I ran all the way to our local market, over a mile distant, because I knew my mother would be there buying fruit and vegetables, and I showed her the money. She could not believe it. Neither could I! We went straight to a favourite stall of ours and soon did a deal, exchanging my brand-new half-crown for a chip-straw basket containing fifteen pounds of Grade One tomatoes. Before the evening was out my mother had bottled almost the entire lot for the following winter. The first real money I ever earned seemed to go a very long way . . .

My four shillings a week was a Godsend in difficult times. Most of it was spent on school uniform and the textbooks which we had to buy for school; there was no school library, and the local authority, Lancashire and Greater Manchester, provided only stationery—no books. There must have been thousands of boys in much the same circumstances. However dearly we might have liked to spend a shilling on a boys' magazine, there was simply no hope of our managing it. But on the twenty-fifth of the month I was delivering my papers and amongst them was a magazine new to me. On my round there were five homes where lucky boys got *B.O.P.* delivered with the family order. It was the first copy I had seen. I was able to skip through the contents on the morning of publication, reading a bit here and a bit there . . . it was not the same as reading a copy right through, but I soon hit on a brilliant idea. The magazine would surely be available in the reading-room of our local public library ('the Carnegie' as we called it after the philanthropist who made it all possible). Indeed it was, and the Librarian was none other than Mr J. Wilson Lambert, Chairman of our local Scout Association. Alas, two other boys, older than me, had hit on the same idea and I had to take my turn, reading *B.O.P.* for a couple of hours or so, three days after publication; waiting proved a terrible torment, but there it was. Within a year, though, I was first in the queue.

Aided and abetted by Mr Wilson Lambert I was even able to read the magazine ahead of publication if the library copy came in early. A very good friend who did much to encourage my own schooling, outdoor activities, and all my reading, he even sent away for expensive textbooks for me, on loan from the Central Library for Students in London—and paid the postage himself.

The first thing I read in every issue was the *Boy's Own Field Club*. This regular feature had been introduced by Haydon in October, 1915. It flourished in his later years and throughout Pocklington's time as Editor. Its prime object was to encourage a love of Nature among *B.O.P.* readers, but there were also notes on pets. The scope was very wide. I remember short pieces on tree study, 'the Amateur's Menagerie Club', Japanese waltzing mice, skin marking in taxidermy, tropical fish, keeping jerboas, cotton-setting for butterfly and moth specimens, new breeds of dog,

His Requiem.

NOBODY cared a bit, folks said,
    When that wicked old man at
    the farm lay dead.

He had no kith and he had no kin—
And nobody cared his love to win.
Nobody thought of him kindly—none,
For many a cruel harsh thing he'd done ;
And many a bitter and angry word
From those thin hard lips had the neigh-
    bours heard.
He had lived alone—he had died alone,
With never a friend he could call his own ;
Or so folks thought.
            And the cortège grim,
With never a mourner mourning him,
Passed through the gate of the garden-
    ground !

But hush ! A requiem's softened sound
Stole over the silence.
            And someone said :
" 'Tis the little brown linnet the old
    man fed ! "
            LILLIAN GARD.

Above: Lillian Gard contributed verse to B.O.P. *for many years. Her short poem,* His Requiem, *was published in November, 1923 (Volume XLVI). Four years later a twelve-year-old Welsh schoolboy, Dylan Thomas, copied it out, with a few small alterations, and successfully sold it to his local newspaper, the* Western Mail. *His proud parents never cashed the ten-shilling cheque which he received for the poem, preferring to keep it as a memento of their son's youthful success. In 1971, the poem was reprinted in a collection of Thomas's work, and was quoted by the Sunday Telegraph. A sharp-eyed reader, Richard Parker, pointed out that it had been lifted directly from* B.O.P.

Just a month after selling His Requiem *to the* Western Mail, *Thomas sold another poem,* The Second Best. *This was virtually identical to Elrington's poem of the same title, quoted on the facing page, which had appeared in* B.O.P. *some seventeen years earlier. It was published under the pen-name of 'Dylan Marlais' in February, 1927—and this time the purchaser was* B.O.P. *itself*

animal friendships; prize-winning entries in the monthly competitions for the best nature note and drawing or photograph; and so on. Certainly the feature was very popular, indeed. First compiled by 'Rambler', it was taken over by 'Hedgerow' (pen name of H. R. Springett) in 1925, when it became more concerned with wild-life and conservation than outdoor hobbies. Members of the *B.O.P. Field Club* could buy its distinctive badge, printed on blue silk, for threepence post free. Fellow-readers displayed it on log-books, photograph albums, blazer pockets, deerstalker caps, cricket caps, and even, illegally, on official Scout uniforms! I owed much to the *B.O.P. Field Club*. A joint effort at a Nature diary earned a prize of a Brownie box camera for my schoolfriend Wilfred and me.

It was at about this time that I came face to face on my morning paper round with the Headmaster, exercising his very large dog. He seemed horrified to learn that I was a spare-time paper lad. Instructions were given immediately for all such pupils to see the Head *en masse* the next day. We were warned that if we did such work, we would risk expulsion. It was, thundered the Head, bad for our schoolwork, worse for our homework. Letters to our parents confirmed the fiat. The newsagents went back to doing their own deliveries while we boys watched them miserably, bemoaning our loss of four shillings a week. But new avenues of pocket money soon opened up. A championship golf course ran alongside my grandparents' farm in Anglesey and since I spent the whole of the school summer holidays there my services were soon in demand as a caddie among the holiday golfers. If you could manage two 18-holes a day, a twelve-mile stint in all, hauling the bag of clubs over the shoulder, the daily earnings were seven shillings, plus home-made lemonade or buttermilk, and numerous buttered currant scones. There was no nonsense about tax and my weekly earnings in the summer holidays averaged thirty shillings. In the winter I used my savings to buy at wholesale prices 'assorted chocolate fancies' which I then sold at twopence a time. A Scouting friend who was a grocer gave me an introduction to the Yankee Mantle Warehouse in Tib Street, Manchester, where I could buy boxes containing three dozen Cadbury's, Fry's, Rowntree's and Needler's luscious chocolate assortments (milk, plain or mixed), at four shillings and threepence a box. I sold them to family friends, neighbours and school colleagues at six shillings. Lest this be interpreted as unfair competition with local traders, my mother insisted that half the net profit was given to the Methodist Missions overseas. Threepence went in bus fares, so the missions and I got ninepence apiece.

Thanks to the Librarian's kindness, I was still reading *B.O.P.* free of charge, and could invest a few pennies from my spare-time earnings in stationery and postage for the competitions. Not all Field Club prizes were cash. One vintage win produced a trio of Old English Game bantams. Extremely pretty to look at but decidedly long in the tooth, they produced no eggs and ended their career as a free gift to a Lancashire moorland branch of the National Children's Homes and Orphanages. Far more active was another 'Hedgerow' prize—two pairs of racing pigeons which reached Manchester in the peak of condition—so much so that when my poor mother went to feed the chickens and accidentally let the pigeons out (I was away that day, playing cricket with the School

With Notes on Home Pets and Natural History Matters.
CONDUCTED BY " HEDGEROW."

XI), they took wing and fled back to their comfortable home-loft in Sussex. I wrote to *B.O.P.*, explaining that they had taken flight. 'Hedgerow' was very annoyed, told me that I was not a fit and proper person to keep racing pigeons, and stipulated that they would not be replaced under any circumstances.

Far more satisfactory were the various book prizes awarded by the Editor for my efforts in the drawing and painting competitions. We had a great clump of *Helleborus Niger* (the Christmas Rose) by our front door and this invariably produced a splendid display between autumn and March. Christmas roses against a background of contrasting red brick made a good subject and I must have drawn and painted it many times, and sent my efforts off to the *B.O.P. Field Club*. Other subjects included yellow-hammers resting in the tops of low trees in Anglesey before flying down to feed. In the late spring they would flock with skylarks, chaffinches and greenfinches to make a fine subject for drawing and painting. When my grandfather took a pony to be shod by the blacksmith near Bryngwran village, I filled in the waiting time with my drawings for *B.O.P.* competitions. As I sketched the outlines of an adult yellow-hammer with its distinctive rufous reddish-brown rump and flicking tail, I came to the conclusion that Anglesey yellow-hammers were bigger than those I saw anywhere else. As a boy of sixteen I dared not voice my immature opinion very widely but years later when I was editing *B.O.P.* that great artist Charles Tunnicliffe (once art master of Manchester Grammar School) agreed to judge a bird illustration competition for us. At his Anglesey home, Shorelands, I raised the question of those yellow-hammers and was delighted to find that he had long since come to the same conclusion. I liked best to work in line and wash, and many years later was interested to learn, from one of Pocklington's courteous editorials (September 1927), that correspondents had urged him to use more wash illustrations in *B.O.P.* (perhaps on the grounds that 'line only'

Above: the heading of my own favourite B.O.P. *feature, the* Boy's Own Field Club, *run by 'Hedgerow' from 1925 onwards*

101

In The Land of Shame

A Story of Central Africa, of the Slave Trade, and the Discovery of Neuroline.

By MAJOR CHARLES GILSON.

Author of "Jack-Without-a-Roof," "Treasure of Kings," "The Lost City," etc., etc.

Above: Major Gilson wrote for the magazine for many years. In The Land of Shame, illustrated by John de Walton, was set in darkest Africa at the time of the Slave Trade. The 'neuroline' referred to in the title proved to be a patent medicine of inestimable value to humanity. The story was serialised in Volume XLVI (1923-4). This book was one of the prizes which I won in a Field Club competition. It came complete with a handsome bookplate signed by Pocklington himself

looked old-fashioned?) and that to please them, he would do so.

To this day the handsome, chunky, well-cased book prizes I won for those Field Club competitions are in my bookcases.

As a *B.O.P.* reader, I found that the fiction of the day did not interest me very much, although Pocklington kept the paper's story content going vigorously. A voting competition organised by him to discover which *B.O.P.* writers were the most popular (1928) gave pride of place to George E. Rochester with his adventures of young airmen (*The Flying Beetle, The Scarlet Squadron* and *The Vultures of Desolate Island*); in third place (one vote behind the un-named second favourite) came G. Godfray Sellick, writer of historical tales such as *Into the Hands of Spain*—Pocklington had a liking for rich-textured historical fiction, and discreet as he was, could not conceal his pleasure at this result.

I was much more interested in practical hobbies and outdoor interests, sport and 'true-life' tales. From *B.O.P.* staff writers I learned how to make toys for my younger brother, bookcases for my mother and sister, a magazine rack, a pipe rack, a fretwork fire-screen; a small electric dynamo so that my Meccano model would work properly; a battery-operated submarine which made hazardous journeys in the bath (and then for good measure made life equally difficult for the sedate goldfish who lived in the garden pond); and a variety of crystal and one-valve radio receivers, all of which worked properly. I fell gladly on the accurate

The HONOUR of The REGIMENT

By MAJOR J. T. GORMAN

and up-to-date information about keeping rabbits, an activity which went back to the paper's earliest days, and my English Rabbit, bought on *B.O.P.*'s advice for only half a crown ($12\frac{1}{2}$ p), turned out to have such a wonderful pedigree that I showed him all over Greater Manchester and Lancashire for years, for cash prizes, with rosettes and handsome certificates to prove it. The magazine clearly had the supreme knack of showing us what to do, and making us happy in the doing. Surely that is the test of any magazine for boys?

Pocklington retired in 1933. He saw the paper safely through Volume LV, and in September of that year, with a last word of satisfaction at the success of the Correspondence Club, he took a quiet farewell of his readers:

I have to say goodbye to all the friends, far and near, young and old, that I have made.... It is a difficult word to say at any time, and particularly so when it marks the end of more than eight very happy years of service to the boyhood of the world. May I ask all these friends to extend to my successor the same kindness and affection, the same trust and loyalty, that I have received from them in such abundant measure, and to add their efforts to his, to mention the *B.O.P.* as 'The World's Best Magazine for Boys'. And in case there are any of them who may feel that they have become my *personal*, and not merely *official*, friends, for once I break my rule of editorial anonymity and give here an address which will always find me, if they should care to keep in touch with me—

G. R. Pocklington, Chelsworth, Suffolk.

Above: among Major Gilson's closest comrades in the ranks of B.O.P. *fiction writers for the Haydon and Pocklington eras was Major J. T. Gorman.* The Honour of the Regiment, *illustrated by J. R. Burgess, was a lively story which opened at an Indian frontier post, where British officers were sitting peacefully in their mess tent sipping lemon squash and swapping yarns. It appeared in November, 1927 (Volume L)*

Above: a line decoration by Patrick Nicolle from The Sea Falcon *by Erroll Collins published in March, 1941 (Volume LXIII)*

Below: the decorative title for The Boys of the Bulldog Breed, *a three-part serial published October–December, 1933 (Volume LVI)*

What then, of Pocklington's successor? George J. H. Northcroft was General Editor of the Religious Tract Society which he had joined in December, 1928, and his appointment to *B.O.P.* may have been a 'caretaker' one, pending decisions on the paper's future. During the twenty months of his editorship there is little feeling of a personality behind the paper except perhaps in the choice of fiction. With Northcroft, Percy F.

(*Illustrated by* C. GIFFORD AMBLER)

Mr. Westerman needs no introduction to our readers. He is one of the most fascinating writers for boys. His magic pen touches many fields, and in the " Boys of the Bull Dog Breed " he is at his best.

"'Out you go!' panted Roddy, his black hair tousled with combat. 'And out you stay!' added Malcolm."

James shot like a rocket into the shadowy corridor, where, judging by the yelp which he heard, his fall was broken by the lurking Harriman.

"And that's that," said Roddy, slamming the door and wiping the dust from his hands. Unfortunately it was not. There was a new voice outside and a peremptory knock.

A PLEASANT-LOOKING — but also extremely determined— young man strode in, his gown flapping behind him. There was no need to ask his name or business. It was Mr. Ivor Dare, the new Housemaster.

"Practising for rugger, I see," he observed, his grey eyes twinkling. "Or was it for the sports—putting the weight?"

James and Harriman had followed him in. They were flushed with triumph as well as combat.

"Just a little rag, sir," said Roddy awkwardly.

"Harper and Moore have taken this study," interrupted Harriman unexpectedly, "but we're really entitled to it."

"Indeed?" Mr. Dare wheeled, with raised eyebrows, and stared at Harriman as if he were some new sort of slug. The boy wilted under

Westerman reappeared with *The Boys of the Bulldog Breed* (Volume LVI, 1933-34) and *An Exile in Vahilia* (Volume LVII, 1934-35), and a fine new writer came in, Geoffrey Trease, then at the beginning of his long and distinguished career in children's books. Trease had already published two books (*Bows against the Barons*, and *Comrades for the Charter*) when his two-part serial story, *The New House at Hardale*, opened in B.O.P. in December 1934. 'It is a capital story,' ran the introductory note; 'Mr Trease was Captain of his School (Nottingham High School), and as he is still a young man he has by no means forgotten his school days.' '*Still*' by 'Sea-Wrack' in the same volume opened with the recommendation 'This is a topping yarn ... a skilful blend of seafaring and Naval Intelligence', and *The Crossroads at Broxton*, by Michael Poole, carried the endorsement, 'The Editor is a hardened old journalist, but he could not let the ms rest till he had finished it.' But the sense of give-and-take between editor and readers, a feature of Pocklington's editorship, fades away. Northcroft kept the paper going until May, 1935, when he resigned on grounds of ill health. The Committee appointed Robert Harding 'Acting Editor' for three months, and at the same time approved a swingeing cut in the price of the magazine, from one shilling to

Above: The New House at Hardale *by a new young writer, Geoffrey Trease, with illustrations by J. Reginald Mills, was an entertaining two-part story, published December, 1934-January, 1935 (Volume LVII), set in a new House at a contemporary public school*

SWIMMING FOR A CROWN

him more dead than alive high up on to a palm-fringed beach. He had just enough strength left to drag himself out of reach of the next wave. Then a great blackness descended upon him and he collapsed on the sand in the stupor which comes of utter exhaustion.

Rob was the sole survivor from the schooner "Cormorant," which had foundered on a submerged reef in the South Pacific. For nearly two days he had contrived to keep himself afloat by climbing on to a bundle of wooden crates,

Above: a dramatic Cuneo illustration to a short story into which were crammed shipwreck, treasure, a shark fight and the 'horror of the lagoon' (a writhing giant octopus), in a South-Seas setting. Written by L. Barry Clifford, this appeared in November, 1934 (Volume LXVII)

sixpence—an indication that sales were in a bad way. In mid-July Harding's appointment was confirmed.

Harding had written for *B.O.P.* in Pocklington's time and in Northcroft's, contributing such stories as *The Sand Storm* (kidnapping in the Arabian Desert with a ransom demand written in jackal's blood), '*Revenge Husein!*' (a young Secret Service agent combating false prophets in the Middle East) and *The Terror of the Desert* (gun-running in the Persian

To let his team down would mean promotion at the Works . . . so Charlie decided to play—

AGAINST ORDERS

Gulf). He had a strong feeling for lively adventure fiction and as Editor of the shorter, 48-page sixpenny *B.O.P.* he encouraged his readers with stories by such favourite writers as Major Charles Gilson, Major J. T. Gorman, Sercombe Griffin, Gunby Hadath, Percy Westerman, Arthur Catherall and S. T. James. The latter, who had contributed splendid railway tales in Pocklington's era (and was to write undersea adventures for me after World War II), turned now to wireless-controlled monoplanes and miracle landings. The times were changing.

Each issue usually carried one episode of a serial stretching over five or six months, and two complete short stories. Harding also introduced the 'potted thrillers'—500 words, with a twist in the tail—and boxed items such as *Famous Characters in Literature* or *Great Men and True*. *Notes from Overseas*, now presented by 'Puck' (such pen names were much in vogue), reappeared in Volume LX (1937–38) in the form of contributions from readers, who were paid five shillings a time (25p). The indestructible 'Hedgerow' and his *Nature Notes* were joined by 'Bywayman' describing cycle tours and countryside rambles ('Can't he ever have adventures nearer home?' one reader wrote sadly. 'He always seems to be in Wales or Scotland.'). *The Padre's Talk* arrived, another boxed item—not one padre, but several, the signature changing from month to month (this came to an end at Christmas, 1939), and with it strings of short features on such themes as *The Way to Fitness* and *The Professor's Den*. There was a definite new drive towards building up a regular readership while giving the pages a brisk, cheerful, snappy air.

In October 1935, soon after taking over, Harding introduced a series of editorial talks, under the title *While the Dixie Boils*. Unlike Pocklington, who had, as it were, talked to his readers from the editorial den,

Above: Against Orders, *a short story by Wallace Carr, was published in October, 1938, (Volume LXI) under Harding's editorship. Charlie Liddle, a popular eighteen-year-old working in the cycle shop of Workshops Ltd, is ordered by his works manager not to play in the local soccer match ('Doesn't do to be uppish with one's superiors with so many out of work,' says the manager meaningfully; he has laid a heavy bet on the opposing team and thus is anxious that the locals should lose). But Charlie plays, of course; and his team triumphs. The publishing of a sporting story with an industrial setting (though this was only sketched in), indicates an interesting shift of emphasis; public-school sporting features had dominated* B.O.P. *under Haydon and Pocklington*

The Editor's address is 4, Bouverie Street, London, E.C.4.

Above: Kearon's heading for Robert Harding's round-the-campfire editorials (Volume LXI, 1938-39)

Far right: The Sea Falcon by Erroll Collins, a timely serial which ran from October, 1940–March, 1941 (Volume LXIII), and featured a popular hero, Flight Lieutenant Barry Falconer—'the Falcon' himself

Below: 'What Is This Television?', a feature by D. C. Ebner published in October, 1938 (Volume LXI), which included the intriguing sentence, 'The ordinary-sized person is a very good television aerial'

Harding created the atmosphere of a campfire yarn, with woodsmoke, sputtering sausages, and spring water sizzling in a billycan. His editorials, readers' letters, competitions, *Notes from Overseas*, the *Notice Board* for the *B.O.P. Club* under the Editor's presidency and the *B.O.P. Flying League* run by him as 'Skywayman-in-Chief', all appeared with advertisements in the supplementary pages which were wrapped round the basic 48-page magazine. Harding brought in cartoons, crosswords, more sports articles, and touches of modernity in the contents—*How the CID Works*, *Behind the Scenes in a London Cinema*, *The Principles of Television*. During the paper's Diamond Jubilee celebrations in January, 1939, it made its first appearance on television, presented by Major Gorman—a reader for over fifty years, a contributor for fifteen; and as Harding proudly told his readers, was seen by 'hundreds of viewers'.

War was declared in September, 1939. The Society promised its readers that *B.O.P.* would continue to be published throughout the war (though the *Boy's Own Annual* had to cease) and this promise was kept. The office staff were evacuated to Doran Court at Redhill in Surrey. There were

• WHAT *IS* THIS TELEVISION?

By
D. C. EBNER

FOR many years scientists have been investigating the possibility of sending pictures of scenes from one place to another with the aid of wire or wireless, therefore television should not be regarded as some modern wonder which has suddenly been discovered.

In 1884 a simple form of television was invented by a Japanese scientist named Nipkow, and later in that year another scientist, Weiller, patented another scheme for sending pictures electrically. The fundamentals of Nipkow's invention were used and developed by a British scientist—Baird—in 1923, and the mirror drum system which Weiller invented is still being developed by an English firm.

The Cathode Ray system of television was invented in

"Televiewing."

act like a Hun. But Jarvis! Ugh! how that beggar can sneer. I can quite understand Barry Falconer flaring up and hitting him, and he's been like a bear with a sore head ever since Barry got away. Oh, lawks, I've come out with it now!"

"Shut up, you silly ass!" hissed Jimmy, kicking him. Andy Wetherell, making a great noise with the scuttle, shovelled some coal on the blaze. But at the Babe's unlucky chance remark about one who, in spite of his friend's doubtings, had finally been proved up to the hilt to be a spy, a chill hush settled on the room. The period of Barry's court-martial had been a difficult one for his friends. Opinions had been sharply divided, and this same peaceful room had witnessed more than one violent passage of arms,

until, of course, the final verdict had settled the matter, beyond all possibility of doubt.

Still, one fact emerged clearly. They were all of them dashed sorry for old Griff. What a diabolic thing it must be to discover one's best pal an utter rotter! Griff hadn't been the same since the trial. He was moping over in the corner now, his nose stuck deep in a magazine. It was doubtful even if he had heard the

"By Jove, that fellow could fight! . . . He leaned out too, and I tried hard to get a glimpse of his face—but I couldn't. You see, he was masked!"

PATRICK NICOLLE

tremendous publishing difficulties—shortages of staff, of paper, of illustrations: postal and transport problems: the risks and fatigue of wartime; but there was some compensation in the fact that the demand for reading material had never been greater.

Harding left *B.O.P.* early in 1942. His successor was Leonard Halls, aged forty-eight, who had had thirty years' experience of working as a sub-editor on juvenile magazines and annuals for Amalgamated Press.

Because of paper shortages the *B.O.P.* format was drastically reduced in March 1942, shrinking from $11 \times 8\frac{1}{4}$ to $7\frac{1}{2} \times 5$ inches. The number of pages was cut, and the price went up to ninepence. In August, 1943, Halls asked his readers which of seven features appearing in most, though not all, issues of *B.O.P.* during this period, were the most popular, and thus deserved to be regular rather than occasional. The list was the *B.O.P. Notice Board* with news of the Club and the Flying League; *Aviation News*, also called *Skyways*, by 'Pilot', contributed by Captain W. E. Johns since September, 1941; *Stamp Collecting; Handy Andy's Corner* (jobs for the home handyman); *Technical Diagrams*; *Photography*; *Domestic Pets*. The first three virtually dead-heated for the popularity prize (stamp collecting was the only activity to feature in *B.O.P.* throughout its history), though Handy Andy put in a good finishing spurt to be runner-up. Halls did not ask his readers about fiction but there can be no doubt that Captain W. E. Johns and his 'Biggles' stories were supreme favourites in the blacked-out wartime homes and air-raid shelters.

Because of the restrictions on printing, paper supply and transport, reading circles were formed. A single copy of *B.O.P.* would be passed around a dozen or more boys. ' "After you with the *B.O.P.*" will have to be the slogan,' wrote Halls when subscribers complained of difficulty in getting their copies. Among his correspondents was a P.O.W. in Germany, happily reading issues ten years old; and I have been told that the Royal Navy used the current *B.O.P.* as a codebook, though this I have been unable to verify—it certainly got about more than we realised at the time.

Boy's Own PAPER

MAY 1945   9D

Far left above: an Adams illustration from Helping the A.R.P., *by Sid G. Hedges, which appeared in December, 1939 (Volume LXII). Readers were encouraged to seek out their A.R.P. warden; to help with the black-out; to dig snug trenches in the garden; to drill the family in the use of gas masks; to learn first aid; to locate the nearest shelter; and to be cheerful and calm during raids. B.O.P. readers were also being urged to grow Vegetables for Victory, turn out bomb mechanisms in their home workshops, collect Saucepans for Spitfires, salvage paper, and even to gather sphagnum moss from moorland and mountain, dry it in sun and wind, and send it off to be used as medical dressings for wounds*

Far left below: a fine Raymond Sheppard illustration to an article by Arthur Nettleton, Dumb Heroes of the Battle Line, *which appeared in February, 1940 (Volume LXII), and described the part played by dogs and pigeons at the Front. The B.O.P. of Haydon's day had frequently carried similar articles (page 93) during the First World War. The terrier is trained to give warning of an enemy's approach by tugging the soldier's coat instead of barking*

Left: the cover of the V.E. issue, May 1945, specially painted for B.O.P. by Charles Wood. I was so struck by this cover that when I took over the editorship in the following year I had the artwork framed. It hung in the office for many years

Above: the B.O.P. *badge with the motto Hutchison adapted from Juvenal: 'Whatever boys do makes up the mixture of our little book'*

Below: a poem by Francis Whitney published in December, 1950 (Volume LXXIII)

WOOD FIRE

There is a log of wood
Burning in the fireplace
With a sound like heavy linen
Flapping in the wind.
There is the hiss and smoke
Of the dampness from
Last night's rain on the wood pile.
There is the flame
Blazing yellow and purple
And particularly blue
Where it won't burn steady.
Then there is the black char
And the white ashes
And the smell which is not just smoke
But the whole smell of the fire and the tree.
There is the feel of the heat
That is dry and stinging
If you sit too close
And the warm feel
When you're just the right distance away,
And for all it's just a log on fire.
You can still see the white wood
That is not burnt,
And the black bark
And a notch or two,
And picture the rest of the tree.

Francis Whitney

What does one do at the end of a World War? I came home to an England vastly different from the one I knew in 1939. Should I take a Diploma course in Teaching, and perhaps a Rugby Blue, and then settle down somewhere to teach? That was the logical thing to do, with a good degree in Geography and $6\frac{1}{2}$ years' wartime map-making and printing to bolster it up. I was offered posts on the *Manchester Guardian*, the *News Chronicle* and even the *Daily Mail*, but all meant housing problems. There was a Press Secretary's job on offer from a good friend, and an attractive job as an Editor in the Control Commission in Germany if I wished to return there. And then there was this intriguing little job down in Surrey, which seemed to offer a free hand in the publishing of quality literature for young people.

I had acquired the sheet anchor of a wife, and we had a son almost two years old. Two more sons were to follow, completing the family. It is not easy now to put on paper exactly how much I hungered for a home after all those years in the Army, or to assess the sheer importance of home-making to a girl who had lost her own family in the war and served several years in the ATS. My wife's skill in obtaining a half-share in a spacious flat in Reigate, and my own good luck in buying a pleasant house in Middlesex with possession in 1948, were the factors that enabled me to accept in 1946 the post with Lutterworth Periodicals (the publishing firm set up by the Religious Tract Society, and named after John Wycliff's Leicestershire parish, which now issued *B.O.P.*). So I went to work in the old house at Doran Court, with marvellous cedar trees in the garden and a small office overwhelmed by ivy, in those incredibly hot summers of 1946, 1947 and 1948, and the equally incredibly severe winter of 1946–7, while we waited for the blitzed premises in London's Bouverie Street to be rebuilt. I could walk home at lunchtime and play with my young son for twenty minutes after a snack of soup, cheese sandwiches or a bit of sausagemeat—rationing was still in force. We could get out at weekends to see the beauty spots of Surrey, with occasional trips to Oxfordshire. Our only fear was that our promised home on the Middlesex-Hertfordshire border might be ready before Lutterworth returned to London—and this did happen, but fortunately it only involved six months' commuting in the summer of 1948, before *B.O.P.* returned to London that September. We counted ourselves very lucky.

In the office there was a great shortage of almost everything. Not even an editorial typewriter—but luckily I had an old German portable which was promptly snapped up by the management. Bookcases were at a premium, but I found a shop which was breaking up war-damaged furniture and we designed and made our own bookshelves under the cedars on summer evenings. Two of those efforts were still doing duty in the nineteen-eighties. Publishing from Doran Court had a flavour all its own, it was like an old family business way out in the country, and we found it somehow strangely unreal to be making up tabloid monthly magazines there. We were still using the wartime format ($7\frac{1}{2} \times 5$ inches). Our ration of paper varied from 48 to 56 pages per issue, of which 20 to 24 were reserved for advertisements. In the summer of 1949 we were able to increase it, first to 64 pages, then to 72. We also increased the format to $8\frac{1}{4} \times 6$ inches, in February 1950, but held the cover price at ninepence (less than 4p in present-day terms) until October of that year, when it rose at last to one shilling (5p)—and remained there all through the fifties and early sixties. *The Boy's Own Annual*, discontinued in 1940, had to stay in abeyance, but in July 1959 we were able to revive it in a new summer-holiday guise, as the *Boy's Own Companion*. Five full-length stories, articles on science and sport, hobby projects, jokes and word puzzles: all for ten shillings and sixpence ($52\frac{1}{2}$p). Four more *Companions* followed, at yearly intervals.

The readers' letters were as interesting and friendly as ever and overseas subscribers kept us in fits of laughter with their queries. One reader in Western Australia thought I rode to the office on horseback. How long did it take me? Were there any rivers to ford? How did I carry my mail and copy bags? He hoped we were managing to feed well despite every kind of rationing and gave me some good new recipes for Australian curries. I remember, too, uncured green monkey-skins from West Africa—the smell was out of this world—and a huge Camembert cheese, hopelessly over-ripe by the time it reached us. It all made us realise how important was the family spirit in *B.O.P.*

My quarterly budget was a modest one and the payment I could offer was restricted to around six guineas a thousand words for First British Serial Rights. With this I set about building a new *B.O.P.* team. It was clear that we must attract plenty of sound advertising, and the Advertising Manager, George C. Phipps, became my closest colleague in the early days. We aimed our advertisements at the readers themselves—rarely at their parents—and went all-out for the eleven-to-sixteen age group, picking up our readers after Common Entrance/Eleven-plus examinations, and losing them at the School Certificate/GCE stage. Bright new comics were coming in for the younger ones, and we wanted to avoid competition with *The Scout* for the older age group.

A magazine is never still for long and must move with the times. Inevitably we lost some of the older contributors, but we found some fine writers and built up an enterprising team. An old Army friend, living

Above: a column of typical advertisements; these appeared in the issue of September, 1950 (Volume LXXII)

BIC

*The young Guardsman stood rigid . . .
his face was pale*

temporarily in a Croydon hotel, sent me a young writer with some short stories which he had read on 'spec' in the evenings. The young man arrived one afternoon in a tiny sports car, accompanied by his mother who remained in it, knitting. His work was absolutely right for us and he wrote for me for many years. His name became well-known as a writer of fiction and film scripts . . . Elleston Trevor. While Elleston was writing

GLES *follows on*

Biggles is loved by all boys from 5 to 90! Here is the first instalment of a brand-new adventure serial by CAPTAIN W. E. JOHNS. The story appears in B.O.P in advance of book publication

All characters in this story are fictitious

racing-car stories for us I discovered that an old Lancashire friend, already well established as a free-lance writer, was due home after years of excitement in Burma. It was a real pleasure to commission from an old comrade and *B.O.P.* writer his first post-war serial, a 60,000-word special by Arthur Catherall entitled *Sea Wraith*. It ran for a full twelve-month, from October 1947 to October 1948; and although it gave readers something to get their teeth into, we decided that this was too great a span, and after that we went for six-parters instead. Group Captain Sidney C. George gave us splendid service throughout my time as Editor with an astonishing variety of adventure stories, all with original and fast-moving plots. Like many *B.O.P.* writers, he had had the great advantage of serving in virtually all parts of the world. And of course there was Biggles. Cascades of readers' letters were produced by every serial featuring the intrepid flying ace. His creator, Captain Johns, had been a schoolboy reader of Hutchison's *B.O.P.* He used to send us presents of game from Scotland—very gamey they were, too—and would call at Bouverie Street in the afternoons for tea and conversation. Some twenty years later on, early in January 1967, he gave a radio interview to mark the sad, final issue of *B.O.P.*; it was his own last BBC appearance—he died that summer.

We were, I think, the first magazine to publish serial episodes from C. S. Forester's 'Hornblower' stories. *Hornblower: the Cargo of Rice* appeared in the August of 1951. It was followed by *Isle of Strangers*, a six-part serialisation from a fine thriller by Ralph Hammond, which Collins were publishing in book form. We followed it up with another Ralph Hammond special in eight episodes, *Black Gold on the Double Diamond*; and some years later, in December 1959, we published *The Ice Trap*, a short story by the same author, writing under a new name—Hammond Innes. Geoffrey Morgan, Henry Blyth, Alan C. Jenkins, Leonard Gribble, Hugh B. Cave, Zachary Ball, Showell Styles—all were faithful contributors.

I cannot leave out dear Gunby Hadath, a contributor of authentic school stories laced with rich humour, who was the only professional writer to work for every editor of *B.O.P.* His first story, *Buffle's Brolly*, was published by Hutchison in Volume XXXII, 1909-10, and his last, *The Decent Old Bird*, was written for me in late 1953, and sadly appeared

Far left: when I joined B.O.P. in June, 1946, I was delighted to find the latest Captain Johns serial (Biggles' Second Case) running along splendidly and producing shoals of readers' letters. Biggles was a leading favourite with readers, and we snapped up serial rights whenever a new adventure was on the stocks. Biggles Follows On began in April, 1952, and ran for six episodes (Volume LXXIV). The young guardsman called before his Colonel while Biggles weighs him up, has been approached by Biggles' old adversary, Von Stalhein, 'one of the most efficient foreign agents in Europe', who is persuading British soldiers to desert and smuggling them behind the Iron Curtain to join an international army

I'm sure that many readers would like to see a regular radio feature such as a "How to Make" series by G. W. Davey.

D. Rolph (Brandon)

I have been a regular reader of B.O.P. for nine years, and am as keen about it as ever. Is there any pocket-money to be earned from mushroom growing?

Ronald Wellson (Tonbridge)

An article on this subject by W. E. Shewell-Cooper will appear later in the year.

My English pen-friend sends me B.O.P. every month. It helps me to get a wonderful picture of how the average British boy lives.

Rudolf Sredsuschek
(Gladbeckerstrabe 15, Germany)

May I say how much I enjoy the regular gardening feature and the cycling and touring articles. I am joining the Y.H.A. very soon, and this year I am going to tour the south-west of England, through three of our most beautiful counties. My one ambition is to become a teacher, and here again I find B.O.P. articles a great help.

P. J. Holland (Lenton)

The other evening I had the good luck to be shown around one of London's greatest newspapers. We followed the front page of the first edition from the time when the news came over the tape-machine through every department until the first copy came off the presses. I don't suppose B.O.P. is quite as hectic as this, but even so I'm sure the Editor's life is no picnic.

Michael House (Streatham, S.W.16)

It isn't, Michael; but Phill seems to think otherwise!—Ed.

Senior Scouts in my troop use B.O.P. as a basis for outdoor work. We like the ideas B.O.P. gives us for cycle-tours and hikes in the country; we enjoy Eric Hardy and the sketching articles. I should like to see more colour in B.O.P. and more pages on art paper, please.

John Smith (Ruislip)

Would Billy White of County Antrim please send The Editor his address. Also two readers from Dunfermline and Hendon who wrote to The Editor but omitted to send him both their names and addresses.

The WIZARD

GUNBY HADATH makes a welcome return to the pages of B.O.P. with this entertaining school story

Illustration by Tilden Reeves

To give credit where credit was due, it was Pettifer's notion. But Lipton Minor, to whom he confided it first, contributed with distinction to its success.

"That's the best," said he, " of having a father who's an actuary in an insurance company. You couldn't have thought of anything brainier, old boy!"

"No," agreed Pettifer, modestly.

"So I'll be Hon. Sec. if you like, and sling round the policies."

"You don't sling round policies. You ' issue ' them, Lippy."

"Good! I'll issue them," beamed Lipton, ready to learn. "And how do we settle our prices?"

"Our ' tariff ', you mean. That's what the companies call it."

It would seem that Pettifer's genius and Lipton's ardour were engaged upon the foundation of an unusual insurance company. Yet nothing could have been simpler in its conception and nothing more benevolent in its design. It was this, indeed, which caused them without hesitation to christen it *The Wizard Insurance Company*. And under this pleasant title they added, in brackets, "*No Members Received Unless They Belong to the Third Form*".

For that was only fair, as Pettifer explained. They were out to benefit the men of their own form, not ruffians from every form in the school.

"Oh, definitely!" said Lipton. "Only Form III. But they'll have to keep it dark. Make that a condition. Because, if it leaks out, all the other forms will scrum up for it."

42

Above: an extract from the correspondence page in the issue of April, 1949 (Volume LXXI); five shillings (25p) was paid for each letter published here. Phill's engaging little cartoons were a feature of B.O.P. at this time. Here he enjoyed himself with an exaggerated portrait of me at work under the trees at Doran Court!

posthumously, as his death was announced on the very day of B.O.P.'s seventy-fifth anniversary in 1954. Gunby was a delightful character. He had been a schoolmaster at a public school in Dorset but gave up teaching to devote himself to writing books for boys, short stories, adult fiction, and also song lyrics, at which he described himself as 'a dab hand'. He lived in a roomy old-fashioned house at Cricklewood but his background was that of the Lake District-Lancashire border; on a holiday visit to Silverdale in 1978, I discovered the charming old village church he had

116

surance Company

"True," remarked Pettifer, thoughtfully. "And one other condition: every member must pay up his premium every week."

"Yes. Each Monday morning he brings it to me as Hon. Treasurer."

"I thought you were Hon. Sec.?"

"And Treasurer as well, Petty. You are General Manager. What more do you want?"

"Nothing," said the General Manager, selflessly. "Now let's get down to the tariffs. I was thinking of a penny for each fifty lines?"

"Yes, that sounds all right," said his colleague.

"And tuppence for detention?"

"No. Say tuppence ha'p'ny. It looks better."

"Good enough. Tuppence ha'p'ny for any common or garden detention. But if it's a bit of a corker I'd vote for three-pence."

"And what do we pay for the cane? Have you worked that out, Petty?"

This was a bit of a problem.

"No," confessed Pettifer.

"Well, considering your father's an actuary he ought to know."

This hardly appeared to follow, in Pettifer's judgment. However, making a stab at it, he said, "Sixpence!"

"Your father would charge that, you think?"

"I expect so," said Pettifer.

"Too much, old boy. I'd say fourpence for four of the best. That's jolly attractive."

"Yes. But what about six of the best?" declared Pettifer, stubbornly. "Old Squaretoes very rarely bestows more than four."

"But suppose he does. All of a sudden. No decent company would limit a fellow to four."

"Then I vote we make it an even penny a stroke."

"Good enough!" answered the expert. "Then there we are, Lippy. We shall also cover detentions, impots and canings by one All-in Policy, reducing our rates to sevenpence a week for the lot."

"That's fair."

43

told me about at Heysham, near Morecambe, with many Hadath graves in the churchyard (some with even stranger Christian names than Gunby). I remember him vividly, dressed in his old-world style—warm homespun suit, wing collar, broad tie and tie-pin with handkerchief to match, and soft leather slippers so comfortable with age and good care that they seemed part of his feet. For some years I was a regular monthly visitor to Cricklewood on winter afternoons. I was always asked to be there by three o'clock so that Gunby and I could have a good chat in his

Left and above: the first episode of Gunby Hadath's lively school story, The Wizard Insurance Company, *published in January, 1948 (Volume LXX); and some letters from March, 1952 (Volume LXXIV). It is fascinating to see that 'Tibbie' Reed's magical touch was still working, over fifty years after his death*

THE
BULL
WITH THE
CRUMPLED
HORN

by Keith Horan
ILLUSTRATED BY DAVID PRATT

Above: Keith Horan's fine short story, describing a bull bison's fight to protect his herd, appeared in May, 1961 (Volume LXXXIII). The excellent illustrations were by David Pratt. Another wild-life writer whose B.O.P. stories were based on first-hand observation and carried the stamp of absolute authenticity was David Stephen

attic study, a superb writing workshop lined with books and souvenirs of many places, with a pleasant coal fire and easy chairs to take the strain of a working day. At 4.15 an Alpine cow-bell would summon us downstairs to a tremendous spread, more like a Christmas party than afternoon tea, beautifully prepared by Mrs Hadath and her identical twin sister who lived with them. I could never tell them apart and Gunby delighted in my confusion. Year after year the three of them spent their summers in Haute Savoie, and on the Victorian sideboard stood a magnificent model of their Alpine chalet. Gunby's French, which he said was a Savoie dialect, freely punctuated his conversation and sometimes his manuscripts as well.

One serial of Gunby Hadath's written for me in 1948 made an immediate hit with *B.O.P.* readers. He called it *The Wizard Insurance Company*. A schoolboy formed a private insurance company to insure all his friends against the hazards of everyday school life such as impositions, detentions, canings and so on. The premiums were low enough to attract a lot of good business and claims were dealt with speedily and honourably. But alas, some cunning young miscreants realised that when they were hard-up it was possible to behave in such a disgraceful fashion that impots, even canings, came more readily, with the ensuing claim to ease the financial strain. Soon everybody was at it, with the school staff furious and puzzled, and the Wizard Insurance Company bankrupt! Gunby said he based it on a real incident in his teaching career; it made a very good story indeed, with extracts appearing in the august pages of real insurance-company house-journals 'by kind permission of the Editor and Author'. This was naturally good publicity and resulted in more *B.O.P.* readers. The success of Gunby's stories depended in large measure on their humour. By the early fifties it seemed from their letters that readers no longer took much pleasure in school stories unless these were both original and funny—humour was the saving grace.

A long-term *B.O.P.* favourite was the Anglo-American writer, B. J. Chute of New York, whose stories proved as entertaining to *B.O.P.* readers as they did to the American readers of *Boys' Life*, our opposite number, and very good friend, in the United States. B. J. Chute's stories were always based on some hobby or interest of wide appeal—such as photography, swimming, learning to ride a horse, running a Christmas concert at school or making an amateur ciné film of some event in the summer. All very well done and written with distinction. I invited the agent to bring 'B.J.' to our office next time the author was in London. Lunch for three was fixed at the Café Royal, my visitors arrived at the office bang on time, my secretary ushered them in, and I almost swooned with surprise, taken completely off my guard. B.J. was a charming young *lady*! She was Beatrice Joy Chute, the youngest of three gifted sisters, one of whom, M. G. Chute, was a very successful short-story writer, while the other, Marchette, was a notable historian and literary biographer. Joy Chute's short stories for boys set her on the road to writing for *Good Housekeeping, Collier's* and other quality magazines, and to becoming a novelist. Her voluntary work among the young people of New York and as foster mother of three war orphans, one Polish, one Chinese and one Italian, was very much in the *B.O.P.* tradition.

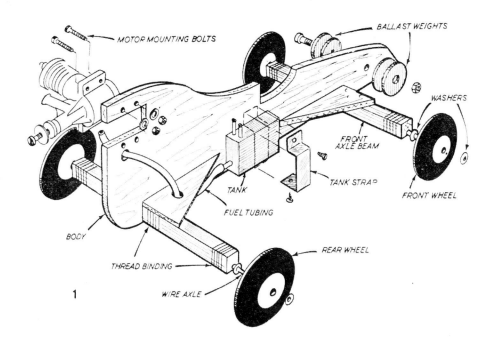

MOTOR MOUNTING BOLTS

BALLAST WEIGHTS

WASHERS

FRONT
AXLE BEAM

TANK STRAP

FRONT WHEEL

TANK

FUEL TUBING

BODY

THREAD BINDING

REAR WHEEL

1

WIRE AXLE

On the sports side we had such fine guest writers as Len Hutton and Lindsay Hassett on cricket, Stanley Matthews and Johnny Carey on football, Freddie Mills on boxing. Ronald English turned in superb cycling copy; and any model made to Leonard Sparey's instructions was guaranteed to work. We built up a team of over forty sports and hobby writers, all of whom would willingly deal with readers' queries.

Turning to science, as early as October, 1947, Harry Harper was telling *B.O.P.* readers about the programme of space research: the giant launch tower in New Mexico, the high-altitude recording rocket with instruments in a detachable capsule which parachuted back to earth, hopes of getting an unmanned radar-controlled rocket to the moon by 1950, and after that a rocket driven by liquid fuel or atomic power with a three-man crew ... Fleet Street friends told me *B.O.P.*'s admirable clarity was such that they read *B.O.P.* first to find out what was going on in the world!

Our regular book supplement (24 to 48 pages, on tinted paper) attracted some fine reviewers, among them the superb travel writer Peter Fleming, and a dear Press Club friend, Ivor Brown, who showed a deep interest in *B.O.P.* and *offered* to write for me at our standard rate—far below the usual fee such a critic could command. We specialised in fold-out diagrams for radio and electronic models of all kinds (by Ron Warring and Gilbert Davey), and, carrying on a theme from the earliest days of *B.O.P.*, canoes and dinghies (Percy Blandford). In July, 1957, we published our first pull-out gift supplement—the subject chosen was Holiday Cycling. Everything we touched on the technical or hobby themes seemed to go with a bang, and these days I regret that we did not go all out for a practical-interest paper, dropping all fiction. In the fifties, mail was running at about 350 letters a week in summer, 600 a week in winter. Admittedly we *paid* for selected letters, which were published in

Above: a special feature of the issue of February, 1961 (Volume LXXXIII), was Ron Warring's article, Build a Prop-Driven Racing Car. *Modelled to Warring's own design the car could be assembled in a single evening*

Below: typical of the post-War B.O.P. was a series of practical up-to-date articles by George Beresford on motor-cycling (May-September, 1948; Volume LXX)

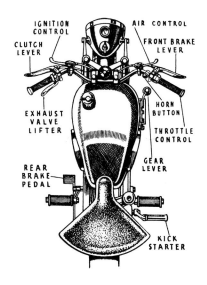

IGNITION CONTROL

AIR CONTROL

CLUTCH LEVER

FRONT BRAKE LEVER

HORN BUTTON

EXHAUST VALVE LIFTER

THROTTLE CONTROL

GEAR LEVER

REAR BRAKE PEDAL

KICK STARTER

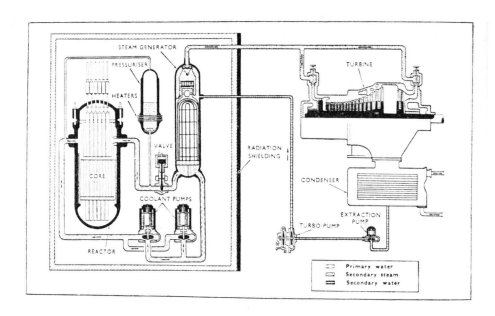

Above: the issue of February, 1961, included our twenty-fourth pull-out gift supplement, H.M. submarine Dreadnought, illustrated by Redmill and David Cobb, and compiled with the generous co-operation of Vickers-Armstrongs and the Royal Navy. A few days after publication two anonymous, quietly-spoken gentlemen in raincoats called at our offices in Bouverie Street and asked to see the Art Editor, Mr Cedric Bush. Naval Intelligence wanted to know exactly where he had obtained the information for the cut-away, full-length detailed diagram which had formed the centrepiece. With some satisfaction he explained that our source was the Admiralty's publicity office . . . the gentlemen retreated and were never seen again

Far right: Redmill drew a prophetic cover for the issue of March, 1954 (Volume LXXVI), a wonderful one to work on because it not only looked forward to the achievements of the Space Age, but also marked the 75th anniversary of B.O.P.'s first appearance and thus enabled us to look back to our beginnings. The contents ranged from Conan Doyle's Uncle Jeremy's Household and Verne's Clipper of the Clouds, both reprinted from Volume IX, 1886-7, to Powered Flight, My Jet Hydroplane and Life in 2000 A.D. I contributed The Story of B.O.P., tracing the paper's history from Hutchison's day to my own, and took pride in showing how, in a world of changing values, the paper had stayed steadfast

the magazine—and boys are realists, through and through. But many of the letters sent to us were never meant for publication, they were from readers looking for help, advice and friendship. We revived the 'medical postbag', and had a very good doctor experienced in dealing with young people's problems. On careers, too, we did real service. Most of all, there were the desperately unhappy boys in real trouble at home or school who turned up at the office because they could go to no one else.

By 1960, there were 55 countries on B.O.P.'s mailing list. We were underpriced at a shilling, but our readership figures were so high that had every reader, or even one in every four readers, been a subscriber, we should have had no problem. But the gap between sales and readership figures, a problem for every editor from Hutchison onwards, was accentuated by the share-a-copy schemes begun in rationing days, and the schools magazine clubs of the post-war years. We did some research into it in 1958, and found that the proportion of readers to single copies was phenomenally high, one copy, for instance, being shared by forty-one readers. Our relationship with our readers served at one and the same time as our handicap and our security.

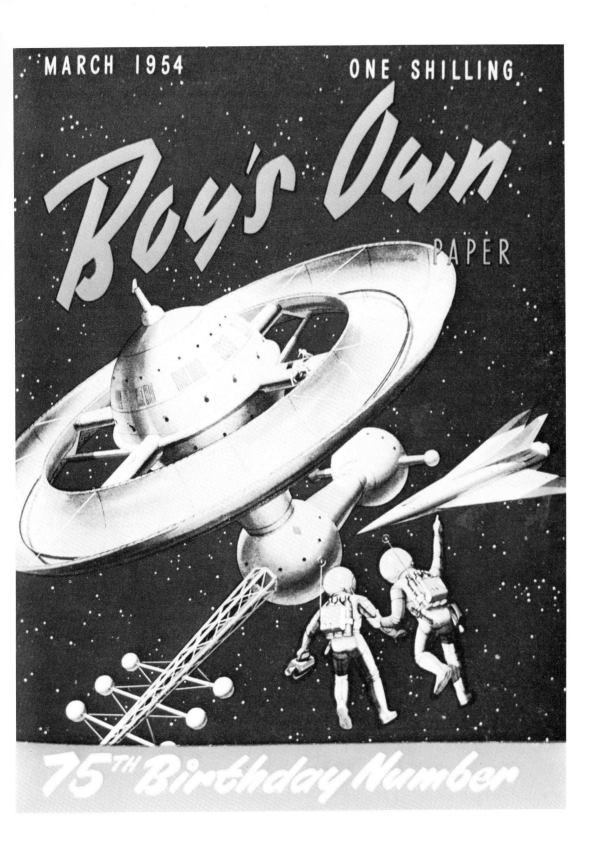

Epilogue

'To be concluded'

TO BE CONCLUDED

Above: a tailpiece by Patrick Nicolle from
The Sea Falcon by Erroll Collins, March,
1941 (Volume LXIII)

In the spring of 1963, *B.O.P.* was bought from Lutterworth by Purnell, which subsequently became part of the BPC Publishing Group. In 1964, while with Purnell at Paulton House, I revived the Annual under the title *Boy's Own Annual.* It thus came back on to the Christmas market after a quarter of a century. Delighted older readers persisted in calling it 'the *B.O.P.* Annual' and I remember how a new generation of boys was puzzled by the use of the letter 'P' and demanded explanations. The *Boy's Own Annual* thus survived the sad fate that overtook *B.O.P.* in 1966, when BPC decided to convert all its viable magazines into large-format illustrated papers, and to sell or close the rest. The last issue to appear was that of February, 1967. I was moved to the newly formed Publications Department, as General Editor of all magazine-allied book projects. A new Editor, Charles Helsby, was appointed to produce a transformed *B.O.P.* in the new style, but it was a short-lived hope. We met only once in the next few confusing months, and no new magazine ever appeared. *B.O.P.* had survived fierce competition from commercial houses, a savage depression, and two world wars, but there is always a new enemy. We couldn't beat inflation.

Events seemed to move with dizzying speed. Control of Paulton House passed abruptly to Haymarket Press and we were closed down. I was able to rescue the *Boy's Own Annual,* which I edited free-lance, often from home, and in that form the title was to live on for thirteen years. In 1979 it was replaced by a miscellany of selected *B.O.P.* short stories in a library format.

The gallantry, dash and colour, the adventurousness, the lively practical interests to be found in *B.O.P.,* kept generations of boys reading—and their sisters and parents, too. There was always something of a family atmosphere about the paper, and whole families remember it still with affection and gratitude. In 1962 I had the honour of being presented to Queen Elizabeth the Queen Mother at a Press Club reception. We had two long chats about *B.O.P.* She told me at once that she was a lifelong

Above: An Interrupted Bathe *by Alfred Pearse, gloriously characteristic of* B.O.P.'s *narrative plates: this was the frontispiece to the Summer supplement, 1894*

fan—and her total recall of favourite authors and much-loved features proved it. During her Edwardian childhood at the Strathmores' Hertfordshire home, St Paul's Walden Bury, she would creep downstairs on delivery day to purloin her brother David's copy, and only give it up to him when she had read it right through.

I like to think that that would have pleased Hutchison and his colleagues as much as it pleased me.

At the End.

SO let the way wind up the hill or down,
    Through rough or smooth, the
        journey will be joy;
Still seeking what I sought when but a boy,
New friendships, high adventure, and a
    crown,
I shall grow old, but never lose life's zest,
Because the road's last turn will be the
    best.
               Dr. HENRY VAN DYKE.

Left: an endpiece from June, 1917 (Volume XXXIX)

Jack Cox

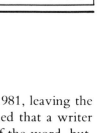

Above: Jack Cox, B.O.P. *editor, at his desk*

Jack Cox died suddenly in the early hours of June 27, 1981, leaving the manuscript for this book incomplete. He always claimed that a writer remained in harness, never retiring in the strict sense of the word, but, equally, his family and his colleagues at Lutterworth knew that the *B.O.P.* History represented the culmination of his lifelong association with a publication of unique character. That he died within five or six weeks of finishing the final draft may appear to some a sad event. Others, however, could argue that such comment is simplistic. Jack Cox and *B.O.P.* were so interconnected that his life after completing the book would always have lacked a significant ingredient.

Critics of *B.O.P.* often fail to appreciate the marked change in style after 1945, apparently preferring to think in terms only of the exaggerated adventure stories of earlier years. Yet in the same way that *B.O.P.* began as an innovation, so it continued in the post-war years to introduce new ideas, new people and new approaches. It was a question of grafting these changes on to an existing philosophy, and why *B.O.P.* mattered so deeply to Jack Cox was that this philosophy was closely allied with his own.

He saw the magazine as an educational resource and his editorial task was as vocational as that of a teacher. Key elements in his life found touchstones in *B.O.P.* The Depression years in Manchester and the Christian element of his upbringing generated a concern for young people which never left him. His work with the Scouting movement and in a wide range of practical and outdoor activities provided ample scope for the material that appealed so strongly to young teenagers.

Jack Cox never lost his enthusiasm for helping young people to get out and achieve something, whether for themselves or others. He resented deeply the final decisions about *B.O.P.* which preceded its closure because he believed they were taken by people who cared little for the readers and understood them even less. He would hate the memory of *B.O.P.* to float away on a sea of nostalgia, but to see this record of its achievement, on which he laboured with such tenacity, finally in published form would have made him a very contented man.

124

Page references to illustrations are given in italic type and are taken to include the caption material, whether this appears on the same page or the facing page. Captions have, however, been indexed separately when they include references to material which does not appear in the illustration.

The following abbreviations are used: 'B.O.P.' for 'Boy's Own Paper', 'cap.' for 'caption', 'G.O.P.' for 'Girl's Own Paper', 'R.T.S.' for 'Religious Tract Society'.